Wings of Courage

World War One Journals of S. S. Robinson

By James Sagan

Acknowledgements

For our aviation books, please see our website at: **www.aeronautbooks.com**.
I am looking for photographs of the less well-known German aircraft of WWI to complete this series. For questions or to help with photographs you may contact me at **jherris@me.com**

Interested in WWI aviation? Join The League of WWI Aviation Historians (**www.overthefront.com**), Great War Aviation Society (**www.greatwaraviation.org**), and Das Propellerblatt (**www.propellerblatt.de**).

ISBN: 978-1-964637-25-9

Design and layout: Jack Herris
Cover design: Aaron Weaver
Digital photo editing: Jack Herris

Books for Enthusiasts by Enthusiasts
www.aeronautbooks.com

Table of Contents

Above: A Caproni bomber in a Rome Air Museum. Note the elaborate "cage' for the rear gunner to climb to the top for a defensive capability to protect the rear of the aircraft; this cage protected the gunner from the center propeller. S.S. Robinson was trained in Italy to fly this type, the most famous Italian aircraft design of World War I.

Preface

This book is to enlighten the world about the American aviators of World War One that became the "Foggiani". All of them have since passed on but their legacy is still here, and this book provides the stimulus to keep the legacy going through this and future generations.

There are few people that know about these special American aviators. But some of these aviators left their letters and journals and pictures for the future generations to remember them and their actions and heroics during the Great War. Unfortunately, there are very few books that describe the day-to-day experiences of aviators, and this book is one of them. This is a history of an American aviator during the Great War that you will not find anywhere else.

The journals of S. Stewart Robinson provide a first-person account, in vivid detail, of becoming an American aviator during World War One. The United States had very few pilots at the time, so the government devised a scheme to train them. The government designated five hundred cadets to be sent to Europe for flight training. Stewart was one of the original five hundred cadets and in the third group of fifty cadets to arrive in Italy for the training.

You will relive his journey through his daily journal entries. From the moment that he leaves New York, his travels through France and Italy, to the up and down moments of learning to fly and relive his antics for escaping camp and going AWOL to visit his girlfriend or getting a good meal or a hot bath. He describes his train rides through Europe and the numerous stops in various cities, such as in Rome, where he pulled in so much sightseeing that he almost killed his Italian driver. Stewart's writing is very clear and descriptive.

But this story is also a love story between Stewart and a French girl. He describes the courtship in his journal entries. However, the story has a sad ending and would have a lasting effect on his life even after he was a civilian after the war.

Whether you are a historian of the Great War or know very little about it, this story will tell you about the adventures and experiences of these special men.

Many heroes lived… but all are unknown and unwept, extinguished in everlasting night because they have no spirited chronicler.

Horace (65 BCE – 8 BCE)

Above: The SAML S.2 was an iconic Italian reconnaissance aircraft. Before the war Italian bought some German Aviatik reconnaissance aircraft and arranged a manufacturing license. The basic airfrrame was fitted with Italian engines of greater power as the war continuted. The SAML inheritied the basic robustness of the original airframe, and continued in the front lines until the end of the war. Later Italian designs offered somewhat higher performance but were not entirely successful due to technical problems and, in the case of the SIA 7B, by structural weakness so severe the aircraft had to be removed from combat.

Above: A colorful Hanriot HD.1 of the 81ª Squadriglia. Italy standardized their fighter units on this French design, replacing their Nieuports. The Hanriot was stronger and had better manueverability at altitude than the Nieuports. Italian fighter pilots prized maneuverability above all and the Hanriot provided it. Only one Italian fighter squadron used the faster but less maneuverable Spads.

The 50th Reunion of the Foggiani

In Celebration of the Italian
Armed Forces Day
The Defense Attaché and Mrs. Giorgio Pocek
request the honour of your company
at a Reception
on Saturday, the fourth of November
from six-thirty to eight-thirty

Regrets only
CO 5-3193-4-5

Uniform Informal
6500 16th Street, N.W.

Left: Invitation to the 50th Foggiani Reunion

On November 4th, 1967, the 50th reunion of "The Foggiani" was held in Washington D.C. Of the original five hundred aviators, only sixty-one were in attendance. Samuel Stewart Robinson would be an attendee at the event.

At the reunion, the Mayor of Foggia expressed his gratitude towards the aviators and that there is still a binding connection between Foggia, Italy, and the United States. In his speech, he mentions that there "a great number of young Italian brides in America, who went from Foggia."

The Mayor of Foggia and the Caproni Museum in Trento, Italy presented each of the aviators with special medals. These gold medals, which the city of Foggia had struck, especially for the aviators in attendance, were a souvenir of this special gathering. As the Mayor stated at the event, these medals are a reminder of "the glorious deed of your aviation and to renew and consolidate friendly relations, mutual esteem and respect amongst us, and to reaffirm those inextinguishable values which make every free man a subject and interpreter of the progressive and democratic world of civilization"

Right: Samuel Stewart Robinson (enlarged from group picture of "The Foggiani" at the reunion facing page above).

Group picture of "The Foggiani" at the reunion.

The Cavaliere della Repubblica Medal.

The Foggiani a Medal.

Above: The City of Foggia Medallion Front (above) and Back (right).

At the reunion, the Italian government also honored them with gold medals and presented to each of them the order of "Cavaliere della Repubblica" for their contribution during the war.

This would be the last reunion of "The Foggiani."

This book is the memoir of Samuel "Stewart" Robinson's military experiences and adventures during World War I. This story describes the dangers and sufferings and courage during his military service and provides a firsthand and excellent insight into his experiences and the occurrences of the day-to-day life of a pilot from training to the end of the war and of his love interest of a French girl. This story starts with his departure from New York in October 1917.

The reader will live through Stewart's writings during his time in Europe while obtaining his brevets and wings and eventually becoming a member of the famous "Foggiani" fraternity.

Above: Nieuport 11 in Italian service. The engine cowling was painted in the Italian colors of red, white, and green. The Nieuport 11 was Italy's first fighter.

The U.S. Prepares for World War One

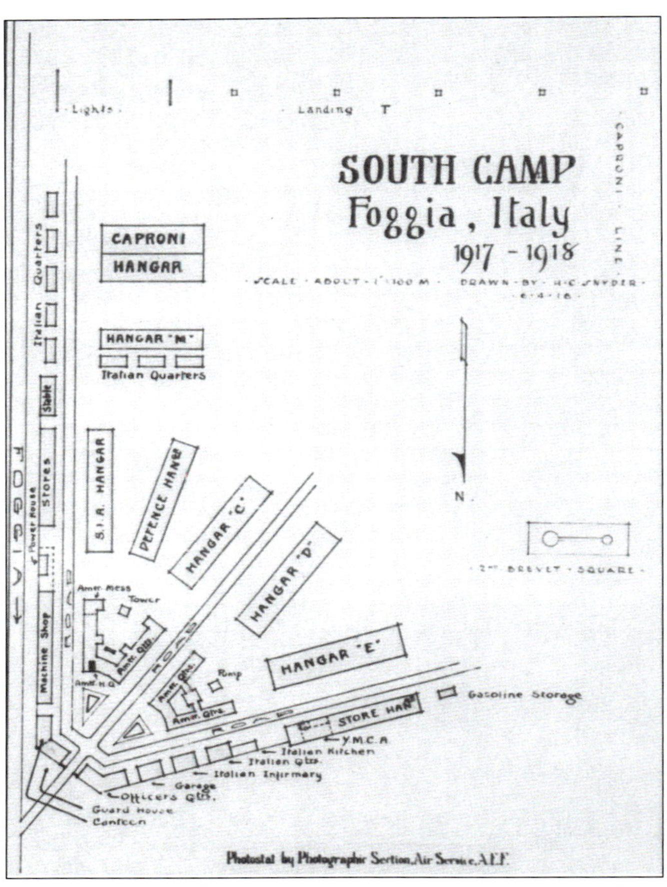

Above: The South Camp.

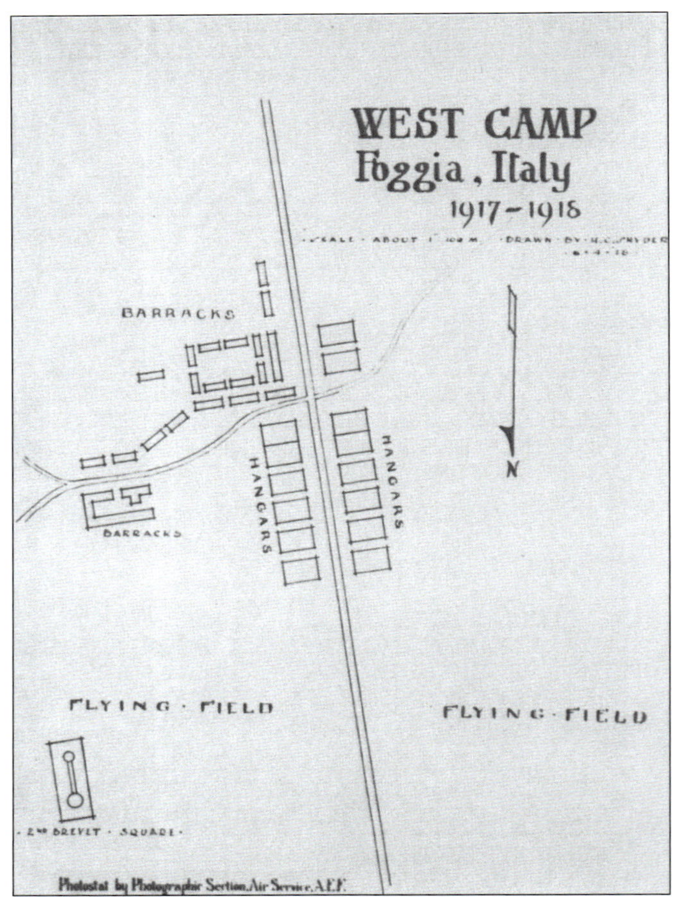

Above: The West Camp.

Only fourteen years had passed since the Wright brothers' successful flight at Kitty Hawk and Americans were fascinated by the imagination of aviation during this time. They were reading about the adventures and exploits of the air Aces in France during the three years of World War One before America joined forces with the allies. As America was entering the conflict, many saw aviation as an opportunity for its best contribution to the war effort, but the United States was far behind in the development of the "machines" that Europe was producing. The development of new machines happened in Europe, with the United Sates taking a back seat. Over time the engines of the machines became more powerful, the design of the machines improved speeds, maneuverability and overall performance and weapons were installed.

But this was still an extremely dangerous duty. These early machines were made of wood, wrapped in fabric, and often glued together with a type of flammable adhesive called "dope." Only thin fabric stood between the pilot and incoming bullets. The cockpits were not pressurized and had no heat, and the pilots faced brutal cold temperatures at higher elevations along with reduced oxygen. The early versions of the engines failed often, fuel tanks leaked, wires broke and propellors cracked in flight. These machines were exceedingly difficult to fly and pilot error was commonplace. There were always rough landings and "ground loops." (Note: Ground loops occurs when a machine becomes unstable while in motion on the ground resulting in a wing tip touching the ground and spinning the machine around in a loop.)

Above: French Farman MF.11 "Shorthorn" trainer.

Above: Italian SIA-7B was a handsome aircraft of good performance; unfortunately, it was a failure on operations due to a weak wing structure that resulted in many fatal accidents.

While each branch of the United States military did have a small section of air service, the problem was that the United States had few qualified flying officers and less than 300 aircraft, most of which were obsolete. In fact, the United States had only 26 pilots and a few military airfields. The United States lacked any kind of ground training programs and facilities. Most flight training was done abroad, in France, Britain, and Italy and the aircraft manufacturing industry in the United States did not exist.

When the U.S. entered World War One on April 6, 1917, a small group of Americans were flying fighter planes for the French, and they were known as the Lafayette Escadrille and had already been in combat for a year. They quickly became well-known heroes.

In June 1917, General John Pershing took command of the American Expeditionary Forces (AEF). He began organizing the U.S. Air Service and set up a large training facility for the new American pilots at Issoudun, located in central France. The U. S. Army Air Service established its largest European training center, the 3rd Aviation Instruction Center, about fourteen kilometers (nine miles) northwest of the town. At the time of the Armistice on November 11, 1918, thirteen fields in Issoudun were in operation and well over ten thousand ground personnel, student pilots

This Page: Italian Caproni bomber on display at the NMUSAF. (Photos courtesy NMUSAF)

This Page: Italian Caproni bomber on display at the NMUSAF. Below is a closeup of the pilots' cockpit showing the fuel tanks that form the seatbacks for the seats. The seats are not present but the frames the seats are fastened to are visible. (Photos courtesy NMUSAF)

and instructors were located there. It was at that time the largest air base in the world. The United States Air Service would formally leave Issoudun, France on June 28,1919, almost eight months after the war ended.

The story of the American aviators and their experiences during World War One is not well known. During the 1917 and 1918 period approximately five hundred American cadets were sent to Foggia, in southern Italy along the Adriatic coast, for flight training due to a lack of facilities in the United States. They would become known as the "Foggiani," a term used to refer to American military aviators who were trained in Foggia, at the Eighth Aviation Instruction Center. Upon completion of their training, the new pilots were commissioned as officers in the US Army Air Service.

Initially, these cadets were under the command of Captain Fiorello LaGuardia. (Note: Captain LaGuardia simultaneously was a commanding officer and was a Congressman from New York and later served as the Mayor of New York City and New York's first commercial airport was named in his honor). Initially, a contingent of one hundred fifty aviation cadets were sent to Italy for pilot training. By amazing coincidence, the site chosen for training in Italy was Foggia, which was Captain La Guardia's father's hometown.

Meanwhile, the American government sent out a call to all the major universities and thousands of young volunteers signed up for flight training. The army then established ground school training programs at several universities since there were only three training airfields in the United States and only a few qualified instructors. It quickly became obvious that all firsthand flight training would need to be done in Europe.

These volunteers soon made their way to the college campuses of Ohio State University, Princeton University, Cornell University, University of Texas at Austin, University of California at Berkley, University of Illinois, and Massachusetts Institute of Technology for an intense eight weeks of instruction. These Ground Schools, as they were called, provided the development of the Air Service branch of the Army during the war and provided a basic education for aspiring pilots but also vetted the candidates that were not suited to be pilots.

The flyer cadets were issued uniforms, given shots, and introduced to basic military discipline and drills. They would receive instruction and training in flight theory, operation and maintenance of aircraft and engines, Morse Code, meteorology, astronomy, navigation, and the operation of machine guns.

The eight weeks of training were intense and incredibly competitive. The graduates were promised officer commissions with only the top men in each of the classes at the various locations selected for flight training in Europe. Those scoring at the top of their class were considered honor graduates and would have had grades of ninety five percent or higher to be considered. These honor graduates were rewarded with immediate overseas assignments for flight training.

Once the Ground training was completed, they would travel to Fort Wood in New York (Fort Wood was located at the base of the Statue of Liberty in New York harbor) and board ships for a potentially dangerous voyage to Liverpool, England in a convoy of ships and then onto France. The facilities at Issoudun, France were still under construction and the other flight schools in France and England were overcrowded. But the facility in Foggia, Italy agreed to train five hundred Americans and Captain LaGuardia, and his staff agreed to use the site. (Stewart was in the third "50" group to arrive in Foggia)

The Campo di Aviazione, Foggia Sud, was located on a wide-open piece of land near the spur of the boot of Italy on the eastern side of the country. It was about one and a half miles from the town of Foggia and approximately 120 miles from Rome and 80 miles from Naples. The camp was divided up; North Camp (Italian aviators), South Camp (American aviators) and Camp (West) Ovest (American aviators).

World War One on the Italian Front was often forgotten, lacking the scope and intensity of the Western Front. The Italians had declared war on Austria-Hungary in 1915 and used their Caproni trimotor machines to bomb Austrian airfields, roads, and railways. The Americans had been settled in at Foggia only a brief time when the Italians were defeated and pushed back by the Germans and Austrians in the Battle of Caporetto in November 1917.

When the cadets started to arrive in October 1917, the weather was still warm and there were already several Americans in Foggia under the command of Major William Ryan. The new student cadets began learning the principles of flying immediately with Italian instructors on the French Farman MF.11 "Shorthorn" machines, which were a version of the Wright brothers' machine. The French Farman was a bi-wing machine with pusher propellers. It had

Above: The construction of the Caproni cockpit. Photo credit: Kjetil Dahle.)

tandem cockpits but no windscreen, so the student and instructor were exposed in the slipstream from the waist up. After his solo in the Farman, the student was rated as a military pilot and commissioned either a first or second lieutenant. About fifty of the graduates went on to train in aerial gunnery and become pursuit pilots, but that program faltered because of a shortage of aircraft, the unreliability of the machines and other reasons. Follow-on training for bomber pilots was more successful.

In January 1918, the students at Foggia were divided into two camps. Major Ryan had overall command and was also the head of one of the camps, with Captain LaGuardia in command of the other camp. After getting set up in the barracks, the flight instruction began, and each cadet was given a seven minute "joy ride" on a Farman bi-wing machine. The cadet would sit in front of the instructor and the motor and propellor were behind them. Because of the language difficulties the instructors would communicate with hand gestures, which caused problems because the instructor was sitting behind the cadet. The Italian method of training was terribly slow and methodical and often the weather conditions would cancel that day's instruction. It would be months before a cadet would be able to make a solo flight.

The cadets were housed in barracks, trained in proper military discipline, kept in shape, and conditioned daily. A typical day was reveille at 4:45 a.m., flying from 6 a.m. until 9 a.m., then various work details, drills, flying again from 4 p.m. until 6 p.m., dinner at 7 p.m. and then lights out at 9 p.m. The same food was served every day, spaghetti, and macaroni. When off duty, the cadets could walk to downtown Foggia, however, certain areas were off limits to them.

Caproni Training

Initially, the new pilots were given a choice between training on the big Caproni bomber or the new, nimble-looking SIA-7B reconnaissance bomber. Naturally, most of the new pilots picked the SIA. The United States had ordered several of the latest SIAs, which offered increased speed and efficiency—but had a reputation for structural troubles. Several test pilots had been killed. The first American to fly a SIA at Foggia was killed when the airplane buckled under him.

Captain La Guardia declared the SIAs to be "junk" and suspended training. "I informed the Italian factory making them that we did not care to receive any more of them at Foggia," he said. He made his decision stick, despite the protests of the company and the Italian government. The United States took the planes already on hand but canceled the rest of the order. The rest of the Foggiani cadets trained in various models of the three-engine Caproni bomber. (Note: The aviation museum in Stavanger is restoring a Caproni Ca.310. The construction of the Caproni cockpit. Photo credit: Kjetil Dahle.)

The Italian method of instruction was notoriously slow but thorough despite the language difficulties, shortage of machines, shortages of oil and harsh weather conditions. "Toppo vento, non si vola" (too windy, you cannot fly) became the term used most often and the Americans waited to fly. On average, there was only one lesson a day. The cadets were required to have twenty-five lessons with an instructor before doing their solo flight. Then the cadets would advance to 2nd brevet training after making their solo flights.

During their solo flights, the cadets were required to make quarter turns and half turns, landing in a small area and finally a "raid." A "raid" was a cross-country flight that was a triangular course to Barletta, then to

Left: (l to r) - Maggiore Fiorello LaGuardia, Maggiore Negrotto CAMBIASO, Capitano Zapelloni FEDERICO, and seated Mitragliere Firmani OTELLO.

Above: Typical Caproni bomber with rear gunner in position .

This view of the Caproni bomber in a museum in Rome shows the rear gunner's precarious position. He stood on a platform over the center engine and fired over the propeller arc. The metal cage was to keep the gunner's extremities safely out of the propeller arc, often known as the line that divides. The Caproni's tri-motor design was a key to its success; unlike two-engine aircraft of the time the Caproni could maintain altitude after an engine failure and return to base.

Above: The Caproni bomber in flight. A tri-motor design, it was capable of flight with only one of its three engines. The Caproni's distinctive configuration coupled with its success in combat made it the iconic Italian aircraft of WWI.

Above: Italian Caproni Ca.5 serial 1222 in the United States late in the war. It has already had Liberty engines installed as a prototype for its proposed production in the United States. The Ca.5 was more streamlined than the Ca.3.

Bari and then back to Foggia. They had to climb up to ten thousand and twelve thousand feet. This was measured by the cadets wearing a "barograph" around their neck. When these exercises were completed, the cadets would be considered aviators and were commissioned.

In March 1918, some cadets were finally given their commissions as 1st Lieutenant's. (Note: Originally, the cadets were promised a commission as 1st Lieutenant, however, General John Pershing and other senior staff officers objected and instead offered the cadets a 2nd Lieutenant commission. This decision caused many of the cadets to question whether to continue the training as aviators or move onto another training course. Finally, the Secretary of War intervened, and the decision was made that all cadets that completed Ground School prior to October 20, 1917, would be commissioned a 1st, Lieutenant.)

Of the approximately five hundred American cadets that received flight training, one hundred thirty-one of them went on to advanced training and completed the bombardment course on the big Caproni 350CA biwing machine. Unfortunately, accidents were frequent and sometimes fatal.

Then the cadets were trained on the more powerful bomber, the Caproni 450 H.P. machine. By June of 1918, the first group of Foggia trained pilots completed their training and were sent to France and placed under the American command in the U.S. Army Air Squadron.

While many of the Foggia graduates were transferred to the western front to fly with the American Expeditionary Force (AEF), about seventy-five men stayed in Italy. These "Foggiani" were attached to Italian bomber squadrons and flew missions with the Italian Air Force. These missions marked the first combat bomber operations by member of the U.S. Army Air Service while flying the Caproni bombers. American pilot participation was highly active, and several flyers eventually received Italy's highest decoration, the Medaglia di Oro, for their heroism.

As the war ended, U.S. pilots on the southern front were withdrawn and the combat division headquarters was closed on November 19, 1919. Eighty American pilots had served with the Italians. The greatest number at the front at any one time was 58 and they took part in 65 missions and flew 587 hours of combat operations.

Historians would credit the role of aviation playing a critical part in the defeat of the Austrian Army on November 7, 1918, and with the Axis broken the Germans would surrender to an armistice four days later.

Introduction of S. S. Robinson

This American aviator was member of the prolific and highly respected Robinson family of Indiana County in western Pennsylvania. The Robinson family owned numerous acres of land and properties throughout Indiana County in the late 1800's and early 1900's, leading to a large western portion of the county being called the "Robinson District". He was also a relative of the actor, Jimmy Stewart. A cousin, Ada M. Robinson Stewart, was married to Jimmy Stewart's grandfather.

Samuel Stewart Robinson or "Stewart," as family and friends called him, came from a very patriotic and entrepreneurial family. He was a fourth-generation member of the Robinson family born in the United States. His great-great grandfather, Robert Robinson, was a patriot during the American Revolutionary War, having fought at the Battles of Brandywine and Germantown, and was one of the original pioneers who settled on the western frontier of Westmoreland County, now known as Indiana County. Robert and his wife Rachel settled and lived on 210 acres near Saltsburg, Pennsylvania. Today, there are still 0.62 acres of the original land owned by the heirs of Robert and Rachel, which is the Robinson River Hill Cemetery.

The Robinson family had many members that served in the military and in various wars and conflicts. The first generation the of Robinson family were all patriots of the American Revolution. The brothers William, Robert, and brother-in-law Samuel Weir (Robert's wife's youngest brother) were together at Brandywine and Germantown. They then became Frontier Rangers along with their brother John on the Western Frontier in Westmoreland County. The Robinson's had family members serving in the War of 1812 and the Civil War. During the Civil War, two Robinson brothers were at the second Battle of Bull Run; unfortunately, one brother was killed and the other severely wounded.

Stewart was born on February 2, 1894, in a small town called Saltsburg, Pennsylvania. He was the son of James White Robinson and Estella Blanche (Stewart) Robinson. He had four siblings: Grace Augusta (1890-1980), James Arthur (Art) (1897-1980), Harold (Had) Tracey (1899-1979) and Dorothy Blanche (1908-1986).

In World War I, Stewart and two cousins, Joseph and Harry Rex, were members of the U.S. Army. Joseph and Harry Rex were stationed near Verdun, France, close to the war front and Stewart was stationed in Italy and France during the war. Stewart's brother James Arthur served from October 15, 1918, to December 10, 1918, as a private at the Students Army Training Corps at the University of Pittsburgh. He never served overseas.

Stewart Robinson graduated from Saltsburg High School and Kiski Preparatory School and went on to graduate from Princeton University on Tuesday June 13, 1916, at the age of twenty-two. While at Princeton University, he was a member of the Phi Beta Kappa Fraternity. After graduating, he went to work as a banker for Alexander Brown & Sons in Baltimore, Maryland.

Then the United States became involved in World War One in early 1917 and he enlisted in the Army on May 13, 1917, and reported for training in the Officers' Training Corp (OTC) at Ft. Myer, Virginia, with the 5th Provisional Training Regiment from June 5, 1917, until August 4, 1917, as a private First Class. He became fascinated with the dynamics and workings of flying machines and transferred from artillery to aviation. Stewart reported to the Aviation Section, Signal Enlisted Reserve Corps (ERC) (Air Service) on August 15, 1917. He then attended The United States School of Military Aeronautics (USSMA) at Princeton University (opened on July 5, 1917) in New Jersey, also called Ground School Training Program, from August 4, 1917, to September 29, 1917, and graduated with honors. He was called to active duty on October 6, 1917, and transferred to Ft. Wood for overseas transport. During World War One, Fort Myer was a staging area for many engineering, artillery, and chemical companies and regiments.

(Note: The United States School of Military Aeronautics (USSMA) was a series of government-run ground schools. The USSMA was an academic program with no flying involved.)

He left New York for England on October 13, 1917, aboard the Cunard line ship RMS *Pannonia*. (RMS *Pannonia* was a transatlantic ship built in Scotland in 1902 and scrapped in Germany in 1922)

He was commissioned and sworn in as a First Lieutenant in the 8th Aviation Instrument Center in Foggia, Italy on June 4, 1918, until his discharge at Camp Dix in New Jersey on October 27, 1919. In total, he served overseas from October 13, 1917, to October

Above & Above Right: Samuel Stewart Robinson, 1st Lieutenant, U.S. Army Air Service with his wings.

15, 1919.

As you read Stewart's day-to-day experiences, you will notice various terms and grammar used that may be considered offensive today but were acceptable during the time period of his journal writing. The reader will note that his writing style reflects his roots in western Pennsylvania and his use of various slang terms and how they are used grammatically and his favorite saying "eh what?." Regardless of his Ivy League education, the writing style and geographical slang that Stewart uses are projected throughout his journal entries. Also, it is important to note that airplanes were called machines which were typical of this era. You will also note that he receives correspondence mostly from two ladies in his life during this time: Virginia Pearce, who was a school classmate from Saltsburg, Pennsylvania and Odette, a girlfriend from Reuilly, France and that the number thirteen, his lucky number, has significance in his life, i.e. important dates.

He will explain his ship voyage and train rides in colorful and clear prose. The reader will live through him on his travels, from sleeping on floors of the ships and trains and in box cars, to surviving numerous bouts of dysentery and the Spanish Flu pandemic. He will rekindle his schoolboy antics of going AWOL (Absent without leave), sneaking out of camp, being arrested, receiving demerits, and doing special duty because of his antics.

He tells of how he had not bathed in about a month from the time he left New York until his arrival in France. Stewart delivers details of the meager food and rations provided. He will describe his travels through the cities and towns of France and Italy on the way to Foggia, Italy. He provides detailed descriptions of the scenery, the sites, the food, and the exploits of having to run to catch the train during his journey. He was always trying to see and experience as much as possible at each stop. Many of the adventures will remind the reader of a young schoolboy running off somewhere trying not to get caught by the teacher. The train ride from Issoudun, France to Foggia, Italy was the longest and best train ride, with stops in Lyon, Chambery, Turin, Genoa, Rome, and Naples. He tells us how he hated to be the barracks police, otherwise known as the "Officer of the

Above: The RMS *Pannonia.*

Day." He will describe his thrill and excitement of his first flying experience, his "joy ride" of seven minutes as they called it, after waiting for 32 days and then getting his first lesson on the same day. Stewart would learn to fly the Farman, Caproni, and Caudron machines. Then he will provide a vivid detail of his cross country "raid" to finally earn his brevets.

According to the Manual of Regulation issued during Ground School at Princeton University, a flying officer is described as follows: *"Candidates should be men of the highest character, well educated and of good physique. They may be light in weight and youthful in appearance, but applicants will not be recommended who are not in every way qualified and fitted to be officers in the United States Army."* This description fits Stewart since he weighed only about one hundred twenty pounds at the time of his entrance into Ground School.

Above: The sole prototype of the Pomilio Gamma fighter. The Pomilio company was purchased by Ansaldo, who preferred their own Ballila fighter design, and the Gamma did not progress beyond this prototype.

Above: A restored Nieuport 10 of the Italian air servive. After the Nieuport 10 was retired from the front it was used in the training schools as was this example.

October 1917 To February 1918

We were told the evening of the 12th of October that we could not go to New York because we would sail the next a.m. at 7 o'clock. So, after a poor night's sleep (for it poured and rained all night and we were almost drowned in our tents) we were called at 4 a.m. and had a great time packing up in the dark with the aid of a little candlelight. Each man had to take care of his own luggage, and we were told at the last minute that we weren't allowed to take suitcases or travelling bags with us. So, I had to unpack my bag, unrope my trunk and chuck a whole pile of stuff into the trunk and into my bedding roll. I have learned since that the bag didn't reach home until several months later and then it was pretty battered up. Believe me often wished to have that bag over here when I have been making trips here and there. I could easily have bought my bag as many of the fellows sneaked theirs on.

I am writing this part of my diary in October 1918, just a year after these things happened so don't be surprised if I am a little inaccurate at times and dates, etc.

To resume my story, at 7 a.m. we boarded a ferry boat and crossed over to the N.Y. side and were transferred to the Pannonia, a British boat of the Cunard Line. There were 77 of us cadets and we were all assigned to staterooms. Since my name is rather far down the alphabet I got a room on the 3rd deck with a rather small porthole. Of course, the officers naturally got the best rooms, then came the cadets and then the enlisted men. There were about 1700 of us altogether on board. There were some 1500 enlisted men, and they lived down in the hold. Taking into consideration that the boat was an old cattle boat which plied between London and Constantinople, the hold wasn't a very nice place to live in.

About 10 a.m. we pulled out of N.Y. harbor. It sure made a person feel rather funny to be pulling away from the U.S. to see the N.Y. skyline and the Statue of Liberty disappear. No one was at the pier to see us embark and to give us a send-off such as the boys of the draft army got later on. We were only volunteers you know and so didn't deserve much credit. I, for one, felt sort of gloomy and from the looks and actions of the other boys I don't believe that I was the only one.

The first day out we had fine weather, and the trip promised to be very enjoyable. We got English grub, of course, and although the food itself was very good it never was seasoned to suit our American's taste, and we had the same old stuff all the time. It was curry and rice for lunch and rice and curry for dinner. Anything in the meat line was braised. The major in command of the boat was a mean guy and the 1st day out he got all of the cadets out on deck and told us that as we were going to be officers soon it would be necessary for us to learn discipline so that we would be able to teach our men discipline when we got to be officers. We had had that drummed into us for 3 months at training camp and for 2 months at ground school and we sure were sick of it. We said that he was going to treat us worse than the lowest private in his outfit and he did. We said that we were going to get in a few months what had taken him 4 years to get at West Point, i.e., a commission. The whole point is that he, like all West Pointers, were and still are jealous of the Reserve officers.

The third day out the rest of our convoy joined us. For a long time, there were 13 boats altogether and it put me in mind of the fact that I had joined the army on May 13, that I had slept in tent No. 13 at Ft. Wood and that we sailed Oct. 13th. Fortunately, I have always considered 13 my lucky number.

The fourth day out the weather began to get a little rough and by the next day it was quite rough. For a while I enjoyed watching the waves roll and the boat but toward the end of the 5th day, I began to feel rather groggy, and I vomited once that evening. I had not enjoyed my meals for two days and it was always a question with me whether or not I would be able to eat my meal and get out before getting sick. Fresh air seemed to revive me always and so I spent quite a bit of my time on deck. The smell of the dining room made me groggy, and I couldn't stay in the smoking rooms without getting sick. Practically all of the boys didn't seem to mind it at all. I knew that I would get seasick for I had gotten sick on Chesapeake Bay and on the way from N.Y. to Boston.

The morning of the 6th day I was unable to navigate and so was down in that stuffy stateroom all day. I had no appetite and just sucked a couple of oranges a day. If I got out of bed for anything I had to vomit. For a day or two I was given no medical attention at all and then a doctor finally came down and gave me something, the next day another came and the day after that still another. None of them knew what the other had given me and so their treatment was doing me practically no

No.

HQ. PORT OF EMBARKATION
HOBOKEN, N. J.

PASSENGER LIST
OF
ORGANIZATIONS AND CASUALS

NEW YORK CITY, N. Y.

Organization (1) Aviation Section Signal Enlisted Reserve Corps Cadets Transport Commercial Str. (2) Cunard Line S.S. PANNONIA Sailing Date (2) OCT 13 1917 Port (2)

Name and Rank of (Officers and Enlisted Men and Misc.)	Organization or (3) Department	Name and Address of Nearest Relative (1)	Remarks
PRIVATES 1st cl	AS-SERC		
Nash, Lloyd N	"	Mr. A. B. Nash, Father 401 Perida St., San Antonia, Texas	
Neale, Charles T	"	Mrs. Charles T. Neale 171 Lexington Ave., Buffalo, NY	
Nevin, Harold O	"	Mr. David Nevin, Father Messena, NY	
Nissley, John K	"	Mr. J. E. Nissley, Father 1424 West Noble Ave. Guthrie, Okla	
Nutt, ~~Allen~~ Alan	"	Mr. Robert H. Nutt, Father Cliffside, NJ	
Penn, Eugene D	"	Mrs. R. L. Penn, Mother 3112 West Ave., Austin, Texas	
Penney, Charles Patterson	"	Mr. Thomas Penney, Father 54 Hodge Ave., Buffalo, NY	
Pepin, Donat J	"	Mr. R. Pepin, Father 406 East Div., Ishpenning, Mich	
Pishon, ~~Stugis~~ Sturgis	"	Mr. J. B. Pishon, Father 103 Mass. Ave., Boston, Mass.	
Polglase, William	"	Mrs. E. M. Polglase, Mother 329 77th St., Brooklyn, NY	
Porter, Paul C	"	Mr. William Porter, Father Daingerfield, Texas	
Potter, Edward E	"	Mrs. Rose Potter 53 Couch St., Plattsburg, NY	
Rynicker, Samuel W	"	Mr. A. S. Rynicker, Brother c/o Rynicker, Winter Co., Billings, Mont.	
Rahman, Walter	"	Mrs. Francis Rahman, Mother Ossining, NY	
Rogers, Hubert H	"	Mr. J. H. Rogers, Father Mellissa, Texas	
Rosenberg, Samuel C	"	Mr. Al Rosenberg, Father 1273 Newkirk St., West New York, PO, NJ	
Robinson, Samuel S	"	Mr. J. M. Robinson, Father Saltsburg, Penna	
Ranck, Earl D	"	Mrs. E. C. Ranck, Wife 6152 Nassau Road, Overbrook, Pa	
Schenk, Alexander P	"	Mrs. A. R. Parkhurst, Mother 500 Grant Ave., Plainfield, NJ	
Smith, Harry D	"	Mr. John David Smith, Father 61 Multrie St., San Francisco, Cal	
Smith, William ~~H~~ P	"	Mr. W. H. Smith, Father 710 Canadian Express Bldg., Montreal Can	

good and once one of them gave me some medicine that should not have been given to me at all, so I found out later. They sure were a fine bunch of horse doctors. All this time I was getting weaker, thinner, and thinner. From 120 lbs. I went down to 100 lbs. or less. Once I vomited blood since I had nothing in my stomach. All this time we had to sleep with the port hole closed because the waves were so high that they came up over it. As a last resort I took the advice of one of the dispensary attendants who was an Englishman and had been at sea a lot and after a great effort got dressed and up on deck. According to his orders I ate crackers and drank ginger ale and when I felt like feeding the fishes I did it. He said that after a while I would be able to keep something on my stomach, but I was too far gone. I guess I vomited 12 times in 3 hours and got so weak that I had to be helped back to bed. That night I couldn't sleep and in fact I hadn't been able to sleep for 4 days and nights straight. That night the water came in at our port hole and almost flooded us. I sure put in a miserable night that night being awfully sick and wet too. I had wished many times that the boat would go down. I really wished to be dead rather than to live and feel the way I did.

Well, the next day another new doctor came to see me, and he surely was sore at the treatment I had received. He was a rough-looking old fellow from the backwoods of Texas, but he sure fixed me up and I gave him credit for keeping me from going to a watery grave. He gave me morphine pills and gave me an injection of the same stuff and moved me to the 1st deck out of that stinking, soaked stateroom. He made another fellow get out of the good room and come down to mine. As soon as they got me up there and got me to bed, I slept for 24 hours straight. I felt sort of groggy for a few hours after I woke up. From then on, I was treated excellent and got cocoa, broiled eggs, toast, etc. to eat and was looked after by one of the English stewardesses. It was only 4 days from the time I changed rooms until we landed in England but in that time, I improved an awful lot. The doctor gave me excellent attention. For the last 3 days on the boat, I got up on the top deck and sat there in a deck chair wrapped up in a blanket for an hour or so a day. I half walked and was half carried on these occasions. I sure felt helpless in my weakened condition. One day when we were in the danger zone off the coast of Ireland the danger whistle sounded, and everybody grabbed a life belt and ran to his assigned spot. I wasn't able to go, and I felt as though I didn't care whether a sub got us or not. If one had gotten us, I would not have lasted long in the cold weather on a raft in my weakened condition. A fellow came and carried me up on deck and then right back down for we were all required to be there sick or well. Some of the boys later told me that they thought I would never see this side the way I looked, that day.

We had a fierce storm which lasted about 4 days just while I was sickest. The crew said that it was the roughest weather they had experienced in many years. One day our boat was not able to ride the breakers and so we turned round and that day instead of heading toward Europe, we drifted back toward the U.S. some 50 or 60 miles. In this way we lost our convoy of destroyers which had come out to meet us when we were about 4 days from England and so we had to run the danger zone all alone right where the subs are thickest. It was reported one day that a sub had been sighted but I don't know how true it was. Guess it was so, however, as they said that one of the boats of our convey carrying supplies was torpedoed and sunk. After a hard trip we were forced to put in at Belfast, Ireland. That had not been our original intention, but we were forced to get to land anywhere because we were out there all alone. We saw land 1st on the 28th of Oct. I was sitting on the upper deck all wrapped up in blankets when we sighted land and believe me it sure looked good even though it was only the bleak shores of Ireland. After lying in the harbor of Belfast for about 6 hours we pulled out for Liverpool with a cruiser as an escort. While at Belfast we saw the 1st American flag we had seen since leaving the states and we also saw a couple boats from our convey which had gotten lost as we did in the storm. We got to Liverpool about 4 p.m. Oct. 29th but did not disembark until about 9 p.m. It was raining and blowing. Another fellow was put in charge of me for I was still very weak. With his help I could walk down the gang plank and around. Our trunks were slid down a long shoot from the boat to the dock and got an awful thump at the lower end of the shoot. I thought for sure mine would break because it never was too strong, but it was well roped and so held.

From Liverpool we went by train to Borden, England, a rest camp as they are called. We hung around the station at Liverpool for about two hours and then pulled out. We traveled 2nd class and got our 1st sight of the trip in a European train. There were 8 of us in the compartment and until we almost froze for the car was not heated at all. The train sure was a dinky affair and creeped along compared to our trains. The officer in charge of us changed another fellow and myself to a compartment by ourselves so that we could lie down for we had both been sick. He thought that he was doing us a favor whereas we almost froze to death for two of us could not heat the compartment up. I think that night was as miserable a one as I ever spent. During the night we passed through Manchester. We sure were cold and hungry when we reached Borden the next a.m. The camp was some 3 miles from the railroad, but I got a ride out in an ambulance.

We spent two days and nights at this so-called rest camp, and it rained most of the time. It was mighty cold and gloomy, and the mud was 6 inches deep in most places. I spent two miserable nights sleeping in a tent because there was no hospital there. We slept eight in a tent with nothing but boards to lie on. Of course, we had our own bedding rolls and blankets, but I mean that we had no cots or beds. The doctor said that I should be in the hospital for 2 weeks after I got off the boat and here, we were getting treatment that was hard for any well man. I had sea legs and was very weak and could only walk short distances at a time. It always seemed to me that the ground came up to meet my feet just as the boat had done. My appetite was excellent, and I would go back for 2nd and sometimes 3rd helpings of food and the food was not very choice for the cooks had only improvised field kitchens to work with. Provisions were furnished by the English, and we ate mutton every meal. There were a lot of British tommies at this camp and there was an English Y.M.C.A. canteen. I loafed there quite a bit because there was a piano and a victrola there and I would sit and eat crackers and buns and listen to the music. I had been told that as soon as I would get on land, I would eat a lot and regain my lost weight in a hurry and believe me I did for I was ravenous and just ate <u>all</u> the time. We all thought the name "rest" camp was not appropriate for such a camp because we were not able to get much rest packed in as we were at night. But such a place was a real rest for tommies who had been up in the trenches and were on their way home or vice versa on their way to the front. These fellows had seen fighting and were used to hardships, and we had not and that made a big difference. Anyhow the people over here are not as used to luxuries and conveniences as we are back home. That is what struck us most over here i.e., to see how far behind the U.S. these European countries are in railroad, automobile, streetcar, and all sorts of transportation. In fact, they are behind us a great way in farming, industries and in every way. The tommies impressed me as good soldiers and are a good-looking crowd until they open their mouths and then they are spoiled for the lower English classes all have decayed and black teeth. They gave quite a good little performance one evening. The 2nd night in camp we had an air raid. We were all chased out about 2 a.m. and ordered to scatter. Many of the fellows wandered a long way off. Outside of some fireworks in the sky we saw nothing.

The morning of the 1st of Nov. we pulled out for Southampton. I was sent down with the baggage truck and looked after the baggage. We arrived at Southampton about 4 P.M., passing through Birmingham on our way. I got my 1st good meal at Southampton i.e., the 1st good since leaving N.Y. We were not allowed to leave the dock, but the doctor took me with him, and I got by the guard that way and got some eggs and beefsteak. We got on board the boat about 7 p.m. and pulled out about 8 p.m. There were about 3,000 men on board many of whom are tommies. While getting out of the harbor we were convoyed by a destroyer and all the boats roundabout were lighted up. Search lights were playing all over and signaling by means of lights was in progress. Everything was active. We spent a mighty tiresome night on the boat. Some of the boys slept up against the smokestacks and all over. I slept on the floor on my life belt. Just as on the boat crossing the Atlantic, we were required to carry our life belts with us at all times. We were on a fast boat called the Viper and ran the gauntlet O.K. One place where the lights lit up the harbor of Southampton we could see the pieces of ships, beds, etc. which had been torpedoed. We reached La Havre early the next a.m. and after a short wait disembarked and walked about 2 miles to camp. It was almost too much for me, but I gritted my teeth and made it. At the dock beside our boat was a boat load of South African negroes. We saw some English and American girls driving ambulances in La Havre.

The camp was a 2nd rest camp and a dirty one. Instead of sleeping 8 in a tent we slept 12 in a tent and we sure were packed in like sardines. While here I got my 2nd shave in 3 weeks and believe me, I needed it. A fellow had tried to shave me on board the boat but started out by giving me a good cut on the cheekbone and so that was as far as he got. We had a good deal of trouble getting water to wash just as we had had at Bourdon. I tell you we were a dirty looking crew. I got some American money changed into English just to see what it was like. The English system is surely confusing with its shillings, two pence, etc. The decimal system is much more practical and simpler. The money all over Europe cannot compare with American money. It is bulky and unhandy and the paper money tears and wears out fast. The penny over here is the size of a quarter and the two cent pieces are the size of a ½ dollar.

We left La Havre the morning of the 3rd about 9 a.m. There were two 2nd class cars for us cadets but the major true to form put some enlisted men in them and put us in box cars, twenty-four men to a car. We spent 36 hours on the train and slept during the night on the floor with overcoats and all on and then almost froze. We stole a little straw in some freight yard where we stopped but there wasn't enough of it to help much. On the side of the box car was written in French, of course, "8 horses placed sideways" or "40 men". We had nothing to eat from 7 a.m. until about 6 p.m. when they condescended to stop a while and give us some hot coffee, bully beef (also known as corned beef) and hard tack. At La Havre we lived on bread and soup and on the channel on hard tack and bully beef. I tell you a bit of jam or of chocolate or anything sweet was at a premium those days. It was 8 p.m. by the time we got fixed to eat and believe me we were a hungry bunch. On our way thru France we passed thru Rouen, Versailles on the outskirts of Paris, Orleans, and many smaller places. We were seeing France from a side door Pullman just like a bunch of hoboes. Great idea for a bunch of prospective officers. I found the country rather poor, quite a lot of woods, etc. and not cultivated anything like back in the states. The villages were very picturesque and odd but of course away behind the times judged by our modern American standards. All this time we had no idea where we were going but we were just on our way. That was all we knew about it. In fact, the officer in charge of us did not know either. They were not expecting us at Liverpool or La Havre and we were without orders as to destination. Some of the enlisted men were sent to training camps in England and we thought that we might stay there too. Finally, about noon on Sunday, Nov. 4th we stopped at a small station and were told that this was our destination. While waiting to get off the train a couple of queer looking airplanes flew over us and we knew that an aviation field must be around somewhere nearby. Some of the boys who could speak a few words of French asked how far it was out to camp and got estimates of from 4 kilometers (2.5 miles) to 12 km. (7.2 miles). When we came to walk it we found the distance to be between 6 ½ and 7 miles. There were trucks at the station to take us out but the d--! Major sent them back and made us all walk simply because he was sore because some enlisted men had broken open a keg of wine in one of the freight yards we had passed through. We couldn't find out who did it and so he made us all suffer. It surely was an awful strain on me to make a 6 ½ mile walk in my weakened condition and when we were about halfway out an ambulance came along to pick up sick men. All the boys wanted me to get in, but I said no for I had made up my mind to make the trip on foot or to pass out in the attempt. I almost did keel over several times but just managed to trudge along through the mud. Once in camp I fell exhausted on a bunk and barely had enough pep to eat some hard tack and bully beef for supper. Right after supper I crawled into bed and slept like a log. The kind of life we had been leading for 6 days or a week was hard on a well man and was almost too much for me in my weakened condition.

My first week or so at Issoudun was more or less of a nightmare for I was feeling mighty weak and just wandered around sort of aimlessly. I was too weak to walk far or to do much work. I spent a good deal of time at the Red Cross canteen eating crackers and drinking hot chocolate. We were pioneers at Issoudun, and it was sure some mud hole with only about 5 or 6 barracks and a Red Cross canteen. It is said to be the largest aviation camp in the world at present with about 1,000 planes and 5,000 to 6,000 men. Our crowd of cadets feel that we had a share in building this camp and many of us did help to build barracks, lay boardwalks, etc. The 1st evening there we ate out in the open and then the next day the boys built a rough mess shack. We ate nothing but hardtack, bully beef, and potatoes for a week or so. I had a terrible appetite and would go back for seconds and thirds although the grub was terribly poor. Then too I would eat between meals at the Red Cross. About the 3rd day in camp, I had one of the Red Cross ladies send a cablegram home from Issoudun. We were quarantined because of the mumps or something and so I couldn't go myself. I asked a fellow to send a cablegram for me just before we left the boat, but the office was closed so he couldn't do it. I tried to send a cable from Borden, Southampton and La Havre but did not succeed. I was sick myself and could get no one to take care of it for me and so that is why I was so long in cabling home. I wrote a short letter home the day after I got to Issoudun, but I was too sick to write much of a letter and also too scared of the censorship rules to tell much news. At that time, the censor was absurdly strict, and one could hardly say a thing. I could give no dates, names of places, names of fellows or anything.

They have wakened up now, as I thought they would, and now the rules resemble those of the French and English. It was impossible to take a bath at camp; in fact, a person was lucky to get enough water to wash his hands and face. Accordingly, after we had been there a few days we were sent downtown a truck load at a time to get baths at the public baths. Because of my sickness I had not had a hot bath for almost a month and believe me, I never enjoyed a bath so much in my life as I did that one. I just soaked myself for a half hour. At the same time, I went to a small restaurant and had some fried eggs, beefsteak, and French-fried potatoes (as only the French can fry them.) That meal tasted better than any I have ever eaten because I had been sick for so long and had had nothing to eat but hardtack and bully beef for days. Twice the 1st week I sneaked out of camp, hopped a truck, and got to town just to get something decent to eat. If I had gotten caught by the military police, I would have caught the d……! I sure did need that 1st bath for I had gone 6 days and nights without taking off my clothes.

The first work I did was to help pick stones off the flying field. Some of the other cadets were doing carpenter work, doing guard duty, cooking and even cleaning latrines. All these were fine occupations for prospective officers I'll say. They even made some 1st lieutenants, who had committed some breach of discipline, get out and pick up rocks for a day or so. The commandant got a good reprimand from higher up for such business. We were bossed around by young pinhead officers who didn't know their business, and everything was done to damper our enthusiasm and kill our morale. The adjutant of the camp was caught later and sent back to the states with 21 charges against him as a German spy. There were several others too. The major in charge of flying was kicked out of the infantry before the war for his pro-German sentiments. He was later made commandant of the school, and nothing has been proven against him so far. He has a very German name, drives a Blitzen Benz (German) car, and has a German chauffeur. However, I guess he is O.K. It is too bad that Issoudun should have been run by such men for every American flier from the states and ¾ of us over here have had to go through the school at Issoudun and thus they were in a position to hold up the whole American aviation program. There wasn't much flying at Issoudun while we were there, i.e., ordinarily there wasn't. But in case Brigadier-General Foulois or General Pershing was expected to visit the camp to make an inspection, every effort was made to get a lot of planes into the air and so to make a big show of activity. It was just to pull the wool over the eyes of those higher up. I was told that those higher up along with Sec'y of War Baker made an inspection later on in the spring and that every plane which was fit to be flown was put into the air and those which wouldn't fly were taxied around on the ground. All for a big show. The chief tester was just taking off one time in a new Nieuport and a wing fell off. After a careful inspection he found that on 3 out of 4 new planes which had come in, the struts were sawed nearly through so that the plane would go to pieces up in the air and so ruin a machine and kill a pilot. This and other things make me feel that spies were at work at Issoudun. All this has changed now fortunately and the camp, under new management, is turning out piles of good fliers and the boys are getting good treatment.

After picking rocks for about 3 days, I was put on guard duty and believe me that was a mean job. According to army regulations a man who stands guard for 8 hours in 24 is entitled to 48 hours off but at Issoudun we got only 24 hrs. off. I was on at the hangars guarding the planes and the mud was 6 inches deep all around. Hip boots had been issued to us, and we slept between shifts (2 hrs. on and 4 off) in the hangars. We were not allowed to have a fire in the hangars at all. We put our blanket rolls on sort of wooden platforms raised about a foot off the ground and so slept with shoes, overcoat, and all on and almost froze. We were almost frozen before going out on the beat where naturally we got still colder. Men on guard are supposed to have a guard house to sleep in. I only stood guard at the hangars one night as my next tour was down at camp guarding the munition hangars. The hangars were almost ½ mile from the barracks. My tour at the munition hangars was a big one and a very lonely one. Two nights later the sentry on that post was hit a good blow on the head as he went into the hangar in the dark to investigate a noise. Whoever was there got away without being seen. Just as I was finishing my last tour one of the boys came to me and asked if I wanted to work in the kitchen and cut the meat. I was in a mood to accept after having walked guard all night in a mist of rain. I felt that it would at least be warm in the kitchen, and I could never get good sleep in the 4 hours between guard shifts.

So, I started working in the kitchen about Nov. 12th and continued there almost without change until we left for Italy. Our regular army mess sergeant had been jipping us all along and was getting a rake-off. He was a Jew and so that was to be expected. Instead of getting us fresh beef and white bread from the 2. M. (Military Market) he fed us corned willy (hash) and hardtack. In those days we needed to hang around the enlisted men's mess just to get a hung of bread. We ate a lot of chocolate which we could get at the "Y." Some cook made pies which we wouldn't have eaten at all at home, but we willingly paid 40¢ apiece for them. We just got sore and kicked the grafters out and took over our own mess. We soon made the best mess in camp out of what had been the worst one because we took an interest in our work. The boys were all pleased. We gave them good beefsteak, hot biscuit, hot cakes, rice and bread pudding, good white bread, mashed potatoes, oatmeal, etc. We really fed very well. At Thanksgiving time, we stayed up most of the night before getting the turkeys roasted and the pies baked. We had a regular feast with some speeches Thanksgiving. We had roast turkey with dressing, white and sweet potatoes, cranberry sauce, fruit salad, green peas, mince and apple pie and French pastry (as only the French can make.) The same was true at Xmas time, only a little more so. It meant a lot of work for us in the kitchen, but we gladly did it and the boys gave us a rousing vote of thanks. Our turkeys were bought in France but for Xmas they came from the U.S.A. We always got very fine fresh beef from the states. About the 10th of Jan. it was decided to put German prisoners in as K.P.'s and so I was out of a job I did one tour of guard duty when it snowed and stormed all night. Then they needed another man right away and so I was given a job as assistant cook. The German prisoners did good work until one of them put a stick of dynamite in one of the stoves and then the French authorities saw to it that they were kicked out. The prisoners were in a position to poison the whole camp when working in the kitchens. The prisoners were treated fine, too well, in my opinion. They weren't made to work hard at all, got lots to eat and we bought lots of little trinkets from them. They were kept in a small camp apart from our camp and it was surrounded with barbed wire. While working in the kitchen I stood no formation at all; I worked one day from about 4 a.m. until 8 or 9 p.m. and then I had 2 days off with no roll calls to answer and so I would beat it out of camp and visit the surrounding country. I would make about 3 such trips a week and surely had some wonderful experiences. I would stay out of camp 2 or 3 nights a week and believe me it felt mighty fine to sleep in one of those fine French beds after sleeping on a piece of burlap nailed to two by fours and sagging in the middle. French beds are feather beds, and they have what is called a foot warmer which consist of a big tick about 4 ft. square and 2 ft. thick filled with feathers. Believe me it sure kept you warm. Of course, I got good eats on these trips and naturally I didn't starve while working in the kitchen. I got awfully fat and weighed about 145 lbs. stripped at one time. That is 10 lbs. more than I ever weighed and a gain of 45 lbs. over what I weighed when I came off the boat. Among the places I visited on these trips were the following: --Gracay, Levroux, Vaux (8 or 10 times), Vatan (12 times), Reuilly (probably 25 times) Vierzon and Bourges (by train), Issoudun (several times), Menetreole and many small hamlets. On all my trips except one I walked. It was nothing for me to walk from 8-12 miles a day three or four times a week and many days I walked nearly 20 miles. One day I walked 22 miles between 2 p.m. and 11 p.m. and then went on guard and walked from 11 p.m. until 3 a.m. I sure was all in at 3 a.m. I'll tell you. The reason was that I had dinner with Odette at Reuilly. I met some very nice people on my travels and had some very enjoyable parties. I found the French people wonderfully hospitable, and they sure do like Americans. I had dinner probably a dozen times at Odette's home and at the home of her aunt. I would buy some candy, cakes, etc. and they would furnish the rest. We had several chicken dinners, and they sure treated me royally. I learned French from Odette very fast. She had gone to school in Paris for 5 years and altho' she spoke no English at all she spoke perfect French and spoke it slowly and distinctly so I could understand. We had a grand farewell party before I left for Italy, and I had to kiss her good-bye before the whole family. I had been in this town where nearly everybody knew me, even the kids knew my name. I sent my Xmas cablegrams from here. I was taking an awful chance on all of my trips for I was always away without leave or A.W.O.L. As the camp was quarantined nearly all of the time, I was breaking quarantine which is a very serious offense. We were quarantined on account of mumps, measles, smallpox, and spinal meningitis. The quarantines were mostly a fake just to keep us in camp. I was caught by the guard once but put up a good story and got by. Another time an officer caught 2 of us but I happened to know several officers he knew, and he knew several of my classmates at Princeton and so he let us go. Another time the officer of the guard caught us breaking quarantine, but we joined in and helped him hunt for an escaped prisoner and so escaped being taken back to camp as prisoners ourselves. I had some narrow escapes with American M.P.'s and French police but always got away while many boys were caught and fined $200, and I had more trips out of camp than any of the 200 men in our barracks. We cadets were sure a sore bunch for we had been honor men and had been sent over here to fly and we hadn't even been in a plane. It was rumored that we would get 2nd lieutenants instead of 1st lieutenants and we decided to refuse them. All the cadets in France were listed according to date of graduation from Ground School and sent to flying schools in our town. Unluckily I drew Italy when I would have preferred to stay in France.

Above: The Ansaldo SVA 5 was the fastest aircraft in service during WWI with a top speed of 147 mph. It was the best Italian reconnaissance airplane. Despite its speed, Italian fighter pilots rejected it as a fighter due to its relative lack of maneuverability and retained the much slower Hanriot HD.1 as Italy's standard WWI fighter.

Above: Restored Ansaldo A.1 Ballila #16553. Inspired by the SVA series, the Ballila was the only fighter designed by Italy to see service in WWI. Fast but not as maneuverable as other fighters and arriving late, the Ballila scored only a single confirmed victory during the war.

Welcome To Foggia – 1918

Friday, February 8th

Left Issoudun for Foggia, Italy. 100 others had gone to the same place before us. No place to train us in France. Too many cadets for their schools. No room in England either. British, French, and Italian missions had overestimated the capacity of their aviation schools. Jan.1, 1918 there were 2,210 cadets in Europe, i.e., American cadets; 1,060 of these were on flying duty or were training;1,150 were stuck somewhere on the ground doing guard duty, etc. I was a cook for 3 months and did about 5 tours of guard duty before coming down here to Italy. We had a few minutes in town before catching the train and I bid good-bye to several French people I knew. Was given a letter by a French girl to deliver to a fellow who had left a few days before me for Italy. I also tried to telephone to my French godmother to have her meet me at the station of her hometown, which we would pass thru on our way. But a "domestique" or servant got on the end of the wire, and I couldn't make her understand. She was so ignorant, or I spoke French so poorly that we couldn't understand each other when talking face to face let alone over a telephone. Then too, a French telephone is slightly different from an American one. It has two receivers to hold up to your ears. So, I gave it up for a bad job and went down to the train. We had a special car for 50 of us. French, as well as English, trains are divided into compartments with room for about 8 people in each compartment. Our car was very nice for a 2nd class car. Only officers travel first class over here. However, 2nd class cars are practically the same as 1st class. Soldiers travel 3rd class as do the majority of civilians.

At the small town of Reuilly I got out to ask someone at the station to say good-bye to my godmother for sure. I had been in the town a couple of dozen times and knew most everyone and they knew me. It is a town of some 2,000. Our car was attached to the rear end of a long train and so I had to run up to the station. It was about 7:30 p.m. (we left Issoudun about 6:30) and was dark. Was running so fast that I nearly ran into my girl (Odette) and her mother about halfway up along the train. The servant had told them that someone she could not understand had called up from Issoudun and they sort of surmised that it might be I and so came down to the train to see. We had been told that we would leave Saturday and so I had arranged to have a farewell dinner with the family Friday evening. Here it was Friday eve and instead of keeping my engagement I was leaving for Italy without them knowing it, i.e., until I saw them at the station. Of course, we were all very "triste" (sad) about the whole thing and the young lady (Odette) almost if not altogether shed tears. She coaxed her mother into giving her consent for her to go along as far as Vierzon (15 mi. distant), but I had to put the damper on that by telling them we were in a private car and that no ladies were allowed. The 2nd lieutenant in charge of us was in the same compartment as myself and as we were just starting out, I didn't know him very well and didn't care to take any chances on getting in wrong at the outset. Was afraid he might miss me and then give me the d----! He was only a 2nd lieutenant from the 2nd training camp at Ft. Myer and he knew several people I did. His home was in Norfolk, Va. Here he went to the 2nd training camp in the states and had gotten a commission, while we or at least 75% of us had attended the 1st camp and were still cadets, never having been in an aero plane. We should have been 1st lieutenants. and should have outranked him, while here he was in charge of us. His name is Albergatti (1), and his ancestors came from near Florence, but he couldn't speak French or Italian.

Have always been sorry that I didn't go into another car and have a chat with my friend till we got to Vierzon. But I didn't and so after a painful farewell, (hurried up to be sure, for the train didn't stop long) I boarded the old boat, and we pulled out. The girl and her mother wished me "bon voyage" and made me promise to write all the time. We stopped in Vierzon for about an hour but were not allowed outside the train. We ate bread, baked beans, and canned fruit for supper. Later on in the night we passed through Bourges but did not stop long. This city has the 2nd best cathedral in France. I had been there once before and had visited the cathedral. Another fellow and myself slept in the same bed, at a hotel there, that the Prince of Wales had slept in while touring France in 1912. It is a city of some 150,000. We spent all night on the train and slept or tried to sleep sitting up and lying all over each other. The lieutenant was sort of afraid to stop over as the two crowds ahead of us had been allowed to do. We were determined to get this idea out of his head, so we took turns, crawling over him and kicking him on the shins all night so he would get no sleep at all and would be glad to stop over the next night. He had a bad cold and didn't feel at all well the following morning, so it was a different story the following night.

Saturday, February 9th

Woke up about 6:30 a.m. feeling pretty bum. Train stopped at a British rest camp long enough to douse our faces in water which seemed almost ice cold. We had time to eat a good-sized omelet at the station café. Walked up town for a minute. Place of about 2,500 people. Left about 9:30 a.m. Had dinner on the train again. Beans, bread, canned fruit, etc. The train ran very slowly. Probably 25 miles an hour. We stopped some 20 miles outside of Lyons. We had been hooked on to a British supply train bound for Egypt, i.e., for Marseille and then the freight goes by sea to Egypt. We were switched off outside of Lyons and after shifting around for an hour and a half we went on into Lyons. Got there at 10:00 p.m. but had to stay in the car until 11:30. Then we were set free until 2:00 a.m. Two of us lit out together and tried to get into a hotel to get something to eat. Too late, my love, too late. The hotels in France close at 9:30 or 10:00 some places as far as getting eats goes. So, we took in a French comedy at the casino. We just saw the tail end of it. We managed to get a little to eat by renting a room in a hotel and eating there. Got to bed sitting up about 3:00 a.m. Pulled out about 6 a.m.

Sunday, February 10th

Breakfast of bread and beans about 8 a.m. At 10:00 a.m., we arrived at Chambery a very nice little town of 10,000 situated in the French Alps. At 11:00 a.m. we were allowed to go out into town with orders to report at the station at 6 p.m. We expected to pull out and to travel all night again, but we were agreeably surprised when about 2:00 a.m. we were told we would stay all night. Another boy and myself made a b-line for a big hotel directly across from the station as soon as we were dismissed and after enjoying a wonderful hot bath and a good shave we went down and sat down to the best dinner we had enjoyed for a long time. The bath surely did go good too for train travel is not a clean sport by any means. We had eggs, steak, French fried, (and the French surely know how to fry them) fruit, cheese, hot chocolate, etc. for dinner. No food shortage apparent here, eh what? As it was Sunday the stores were all closed, i.e., the larger ones. We looked around for a taxi but found out that there was only one in town and some of our boys already had it. So, the two of us got a "voiture" or carriage and spent a couple of hours taking in the sights. Pretty reasonable rate, 5 francs. Guess that was "beaucoup" for the cabman who usually sees a few "sous" instead of francs. The Europeans were prepared for the rich Americans, but the French did not charge more than 1 ½ prices. The "Wops" charge 3 prices if they can get away with it. We made a complete tour of the town. Not much to see except a few monuments, statues, and mountains. One mountain especially was really beautiful. On top of it was a golden cross which from a distance looked to be about the size of a man but which really was 100 ft. high. Another thing of interest was an immense palace formerly of the Duke of Savoy but at present a hospital. It was really very fine and as most French palaces or chateaus was a village in itself with its own little chapel or church, its own bakery, etc. There is always the palace itself with many smaller buildings, usually one story, for the tenants. After our little trip we took a long walk or "promenade" as the French say. That is the favorite outdoor sport of the French and of all Europeans on Sunday p.m. The class of French people in this town seemed very good indeed. I purchased a vest pocket kodak (Eastman) and a few films here. Kodak costs 61 francs which at the present rate of exchange is about $11.00, the same camera can be bought in the states for $6.50. everything modern and up to date comes from the states it seems and import duties make them cost more over here. After enjoying another good meal of eggs and taking a little walk we went to bed. We looked over the moving picture houses but did not go to any. Some of the boys met the wife of one of the Roosevelt boys. She is over here in Red Cross work. Did not see her myself.

Monday, February 11th

Up at 6:00 a.m. and went up town to try to buy some things. Couldn't get a money belt or a Sam Brownie to suit me. We reported at the station at 9:00, pitched pennies, etc. until about 11:30, when we finally got under way. The slowness of Europeans gets on an American's nerve. Oh! Yes, I almost forgot. Yesterday (Feb. 10) at 5 p.m. I sent a postcard home, one to Virginia and a couple of other cards. Also, a cable home, giving my new address. Did not know whether they would even get by the censor but guess they did, at least the cable. Have sent several cables but this one made the record time. From Sun. eve at 5 until Tues. (Feb.12) a.m. early. Pretty fast, 36 hrs. Most cables take 5 days at least in war times. Then to a letter from home written Tues. Feb. 12 got to me Mar. 3rd. 19 days; not bad at all.

Nothing of especial interest happened today. We were passing through beautiful country; right in the midst of the French Alps and the temperature was quite a bit lower than usual. Usual lunch and supper on the train. Yesterday we stopped for a few minutes in Aix-les-Bains. It is a beautiful summer resort with fine hotels, etc. It has been taken over by the American gov't and is being used for men on leave i.e., for enlisted men. They are required to go there if they are on service in France. 7 days' leave every 4 months is the rule. We understood there were 17 theatres with American and English talent and all the hotels were taken over by our gov't. There are tennis courts, baseball diamonds, basketball courts, a lake for swimming, etc. All this is under the auspices of the Y.M.C.A. and Red Cross.

About 8 o'clock this evening we passed through what is said to be the longest tunnel in the world (12 miles). It was mighty well-guarded at both ends for fear of someone carrying explosives in. This tunnel is very important as it is on the main line from France to Italy and many troops are moved back and forth along this route. At the end of the tunnel toward Italy is the town of Modane. It is right on the border and here all passports, baggage, etc. are examined. Of course, our passports didn't have to be examined, and the lieutenant dissuaded them from looking through our baggage. We had a private baggage car too and didn't want it disturbed. Some of us got some money changed at the station at the rate of 1.49 lira to 1 franc. In peace times the franc and the lira have the same value, but Italian money had depreciated more than French. I only got 25 francs changed to have some Italian money to look at. Such places usually do not give a good rate of exchange. We saw quite a few English officers and tommies here. In fact, we had seen quite a few all along the route. I talked to one English officer who was on his way to the funeral of his brother who had been killed flying over the lines. He himself was attending a naval aviation school in Italy. We hopped on the train again and slept packed in like sardines for another night.

Tuesday, February 12th

During last night we passed through Alessandria (Italy), which was said to be a beautiful city; but as I was in the land of nod at the time, I could not appreciate its beauty. At about 3:30 a.m. we arrived at Turin. Got out of train about 4 and a couple of us picked up the 1st "carozza" (as the Italians say) and lit out for a hotel. The 1st one we stopped at was full up, but managed to get into the next one we went to. We went to bed shortly after 4 and got up again about 9, had a little breakfast in the room and started out to see a little of the town. I bought 25 films for my kodak, and I had about 600 francs changed into lira at the rate of 1.50 lira per franc. We found the stores very good, and the bank seemed to do business rather swiftly and efficiently. Hotels too were well furnished and up to date. Left Turin about 11 a.m. Scenery along the route is very picturesque. Lots of card playing, etc. on the train. Ate dinner and supper on the train. Passed through Pisa in the p.m. and we got a very good view of the famous "Leaning Tower" and other very fine-looking buildings. I almost missed the train while buying some postcards in the station. We pulled into Genoa about 7:30 p.m. Quite a few of us put up at the Hotel Savoia, a very nice place. After washing up we set out to find a café called the "20th of Sept." Asked a couple of British tommies and they didn't know where it was. Asked several Italians but didn't seem to be able to locate it. After much wandering we found a café which looked pretty good. Went in and found they had pretty good music, etc. but not much to eat and that's what we were looking for. Saw 3 or 4 American sailors who seemed mighty glad to see us. We discussed matters at some length. They had left N.Y. about Jan. 5th and gave us quite a bit of late dope. Their ship had been attacked by 5 or 6 submarines but got away. Some of the girls tried to converse with us. We were really quite a curiosity as we were the 1st American soldiers to stop at Genoa. We soon left this place and went to another café. This café was called the "Olympia" and is not all over Europe. It was originally built for a theatre but due to lack of exits was condemned by the authorities and was turned into a café. It is about 300 or 350 ft. in diameter and has a nice big stage and a dandy orchestra. The eats are wonderful. Good tender steak, all kinds of vegetables, regular American brick ice cream with nuts in it. The orchestra played everything we requested such as "For Me and My Girl." Selections from the "Century Girl," "The Rosary," etc. Of course, a small collection was necessary. We met some Red Cross and Y.M.C.A. workers who treated us fine. An American sailor ate at our table as did the lieutenant in charge of us. Saw several English officers there.

The class of people was fine. Also met a captain and lieutenant-commander in our navy there. We seemed to be the center of attraction, and we noticed several society women directing their opera glasses, at us. After a very enjoyable evening we retired about 12 o'clock.

Wednesday, February 13th

Up at 4 a.m. and started to the station. A couple of us got to the wrong station and then only had a few minutes to get clear across the town to the other station. Walked part way and got a cab part way and finally reached the station just in time to catch the train. We pulled out at 5:30 a.m. Travelled all day again through beautiful country. After seeing so much fine scenery one does not appreciate that, which is really excellent. Nothing of especial interest today. Several stops; one long enough to allow us to get some eggs for breakfast. One thing we noticed was that Italian trains went quite a bit faster than French ones and there were not nearly so many delays. All along the line people waved at us. Very funny but the Italians don't wave with their whole arm but just with the hand proper, shaking it at the wrist. It looks very queer until one gets used to it. Also, when an Italian wants a person to come toward him, he motions you away moving the palm of his hand away from his body. You can't tell what he does really mean.

We travelled further today than any other day on the trip, from Genoa to Rome. We arrived at Rome about 9 p.m. Got away from the station shortly after10 p.m. and went straight to the hotel. We stopped at the Hotel Regina, one of the two best in town. They cater to English especially and they talk that language. We saw lots of English officers and English civilians (a few) there. Too late to get anything to eat. All restaurants, etc. close up at 10 p.m. We were almost starved, but we had to go to bed hungry. My bunkie and myself took a good hot bath apiece and crawled into bed about 12:30 and enjoyed a wonderful sleep until 8:30 a.m.

Thursday, February 14th

After making our morning toilet we enjoyed a very good breakfast and set out to see the town. We looked over the stores trying to buy goggles, boots, Sam Brown belts, etc. Could find none of the above but some of us left orders for Sam Browns and triplex goggles at "Old England." This is the name given to the chain of stores run by English people. There is one in Paris, one in London, one here at Rome and several others in France. They are good stores and keep most everything in the military line, also quite a bit of sporting goods. After 5 p.m. they sell American ice cream and soda water, but we didn't get around to them. I bought a money belt and some toilet articles, and they sent them around to the hotel, regular N.Y. style. It was about 11:30 now. Ern Caldwell (2), another boy and myself hired a cab and started out to see the sights. Our driver spoke French; I understand French quite a bit the 3rd boy with us is a Frenchman i.e., his father and mother speak nothing but French in their home in Michigan. So, he speaks French as well as he does English.

The 1st place of interest pointed out to us was the royal palace. It looked very good from the outside but of course we couldn't get in. We passed the chamber of Deputies and the Senate chamber. Both these places are old palaces used formerly by the wealthy Romans as private residences. We also passed several interesting statues and columns, all named after the Roman emperors or Italian kings. We also passed the Palace of Justice. It is surely one fine piece of architecture and is shaped a good deal like the Pennsylvania Stations in Washington and N.Y., only it is larger than I believe. It is a very massive looking building. We had a very good view of the Victor Emmanuel Memorial. Very fine and somewhat like the Lincoln Memorial in Washington. Next, we drove to the Vatican and St. Peter's. Here we had the driver stop and we got a guide who spoke French and broken English. His price was 20 liras. We spent about 2 hours here and then didn't see 1/10 of all there was to see. We visited the Treasury of the Vatican where are kept all the different gifts and presents given to the pope from time to time by kings, queens, princes, etc. Here we saw the largest ruby in the world, probably the size of 3 closed fists. We saw oodles of jewels of all kinds and descriptions. Great big diamonds. We saw there the cloak of Charlemagne and of many famous ancient rulers and potentates. Can't just remember the names now. Of course, we saw all kinds of famous Greek and Roman statuary. These were very interesting to me as I had studied Ancient Greek and Roman history, some mythology and had read a lot about Roman and Greek heroes in Latin and Greek. We also viewed the original paintings of Raphael. The "Ascension," probably his most famous one, is surely beautiful. Also visited the room where they left the work done by Michaelangelo. Really there were so many beautiful and wonderful things to see that we couldn't see even a very small part of them. All sorts of famous inscriptions, etc.

We also visited different rooms occupied at one time or another by the popes.
We next went to St. Peter's cathedral, the largest church in the world. The paintings in the dome are by Raphael and the whole affair is massive and really wonderful to behold. One statue is of St. Peter and there is a continual flow of people who come to worship and kiss St. Peter's foot. All around are the tombs of the different popes and some of the cardinals. After spending about two hours at these two places we got out of the old cab again and started on our way. Ordinarily we would have been mighty hungry by now, but we were seeing so many things that we didn't have time to think of eating. The old guide who took us thru the Vatican and St. Peter's said we almost killed him and believe me we did go some for we had to make hay while the sun was shining.
The driver took us past the Pantheon where two ancient emperors lie buried. We also passed the four Forums and the Triumphed Arch. We went along the old Appian Way to the Catacombs where lie buried some million and a half of the martyred Christians. Before going down the guide gives each person a small candle (lighted). The catacombs are just like a large apartment house under the ground, there being one story upon another. So far only about 200,000 bodies have been excavated. Here the martyred popes held mass when driven out of the cathedral. Each Christian family had its own compartment with sort of graves dug in the sides of the wall. The body was 1st wrapped in cloth of some sort which contained embalming fluid. Then, after the body was put in, the grave was sealed with a marble slab, which was cemented in. some of the original cement was still there without a crack in it. I saw a couple of bodies on which the original hair could be seen plainly. The Christians would go at night and steal away the bones of their friends and relatives after they had chewed to pieces by the wild animals in the colosseum. At the time of the invasion of Rome by the Goths or Vandals they broke open many of the tombs and stole the jewels, etc.
Next, we visited the colosseum and saw where they had the fights between the gladiators and wild beasts. Here also the Christians were thrown to the lions, etc. The building is immense and is shaped like our athletic stadia in the states, circular and tier above tier of seats. It is said to have seated 75,000 people. At times water was left in the enclosure and they would have a mock naval battel. We also saw Nero's private entrance and box. There is also a private passage from the palatine hill to the coliseum used by the old emperors. They tried to pawn off some coins on us which were said to be the original issued by Augustus or Caesar. But we didn't bite. You have to be very careful or the guides, etc., will rook you as badly in Rome as at Niagara Falls. They have been spoiled by American and English tourists. After six- or seven-hours sightseeing, we went to a hotel and enjoyed a fine meal. Then we went around to a café for a while and went to the station about 9:30 p.m. We left about 10:30 p.m. and spent another night on the train.
Of course, all the time we stopped in these different towns we had to leave a guard for the car or rather for the baggage car. It was done alphabetically, and we stood guard for an hour or two at a time. My turn came at Genoa but one of the boys didn't care to stay up town so I agreed to pay for his supper if he would stand my tour. So, I didn't have to do any guard duty the whole way down. Eight fellows missed the train at Genoa but caught up to us at Rome. The lieutenant was very worried about them, and they had to stand guard all one day and night in Naples for punishment. Ern Caldwell (2) missed the train at some town in France but caught a fast train and found us again at the next stop. The lieutenant didn't even know he had been left.

Friday, February 15th

We left Rome last night expecting to reach Foggia, our destination about noon today but due to some mistake the Italians failed to switch our car off at Casserta, a junction near Naples. The lieutenant was very worried about it, because we couldn't get a train out until the next a.m. There was a train about 1 p.m. but that would have gotten us to Foggia about 10 p.m. no time at all to land in camp with a bunch of men. So, the lieutenant telephoned to Foggia to fix it up. The commandant asked him what he was doing in Naples, and he said that he was sure he didn't know. He fixed things up O.K., however.
One of the fellows in the crowd had been to Naples before and he recommended a hotel as being very good. So about 30 of us packed into cabs about 7:30 a.m. and started. It took us just 55 minutes to get to the foot of an elevator leading up some 400 ft. through a mountain to the hotel. It only carried 10 at a time so the last of us had to wait 15 or 20 min. more. We sure were disgusted when we finally arrived there, and it was raining something fierce. The hotel looked pretty good but was sort of run down. I imagine that in peace times it is a very

good place but due to lack of tourists its trade is almost nothing now. I noticed probably a half dozen boarders and the hotel would accommodate about 300 or 400. We were told that Carnegie, Rockefeller, Roosevelt, the Drexel's, and other big Americans had stopped there. It seemed to be exclusively for tourists and in peace times and in the summer is probably very fine. There was a dandy veranda for dancing, etc. We had a wonderful view of the bay of Naples, Mt. Vesuvius, and Pompeii. The harbor is surely a fine one. None of us went over to Pompeii because of the rain and because you have to take a train away out around the bay, and it takes a good deal of time. I ate breakfast at about 10 a.m. and decided to go to a downtown hotel so I could sleep a little longer in the morning for we had to be at the station at 5:30 a.m. So, I put up at the Geneva a very good hotel, and had dinner about 1 p.m.

Spent a couple of hours looking around the stores. Couldn't get a pair of boots or gloves nor a Sam Brown belt. Did find an excellent chamois skin money belt and bought it. Also, bought a little cheap grip. Then I got a haircut, shave, and massage and went to a moving picture show. Another boy and myself had dinner at the Café Umberto and to be the best in the town. This café is in the largest arcade in the world. The arcade contains stores, several cafes, candy stores, moving picture shows, etc. The 2nd largest arcade in the world is in Cleveland. After dinner we went to the theater and heard some fairly good music, but the Italians can't dance like Americans. As we were going into the theater a big bunch of stones fell from above the theater door. They just missed us. No one at all was hurt. It was very windy.

Saturday, February 16th

We got up about 4:30 a.m. and hiked out for the station without getting any breakfast. At the station I got a cup of coffee and bought some oranges and crackers which I ate on the train. At about 6:30 a.m. we started on the last leg of our journey.

Naples is the largest city in Italy; about 800,000. Rome has about 500,000, Milan about the same number. Turin and Genoa about 300,000 or 400,000 and Florence a couple of hundred thousand.

Today it snowed and rained and was mighty cold, especially up in the mountains. The boys who had gone down to Italy ahead of us had written back that it was so hot at Foggia that they were wearing B.V.D.'s in Jan. and that it was so hot that they couldn't stay out in the sun at noon time. And here we got into a snowstorm and were freezing. We always had been out of luck, however, and we were used to it. The old engine stalled on the side of a mountain and then again in a tunnel. We passed through Casserta which looked very good. There is a fine big hospital there, i.e., it is one now and was formerly a famous school for nuns. We bought a bunch of hard-boiled eggs at some small station. Guess I ate about 6 of them.

After a slow, tiresome journey we arrived at Foggia about 6:00 p.m. We cleaned out the car and got all the baggage out. It was mighty cold and about 3 inches of snow on the ground here in the much-heralded sunny Italy. After a cold wait of ¾ of an hour we were taken to Campo Ovest (West) in "camions" or auto trucks. Arrived there, got washed up and ate a meal of macaroni and eggs. Spent a half hour chatting with friends who had come down ahead of us. They all told us that it was a great place and that they had started to fly right away. Nothing to do but fly, so they said. We found out that we had had the longest and best trip down. We were the only bunch to stop at Genoa and Naples and we had longer in Rome than any other bunch. We were the 3rd "50" to come down from France.

At Lyons we had 6 hours; at Chambery 22 hours; at Turin 6 hours; at Genoa 11 hours; at Rome 24 hours; at Naples 24 hours. The trip cost me $100 or a little better; not bad at all for such a good trip. We hit the bay about 9:30 and were glad to be here at last. We had stone barracks and small iron beds with good mattresses and a pillow apiece. We were given 2 blankets and two sheets apiece. I had 3 blankets with me and with 5 blankets and a heavy overcoat I managed to keep from freezing her in sunny Italy. Our trunks and baggage came out along with us and we got our things all placed before going to bed.

Sunday, February 17th

Due to the bad weather, we were allowed to sleep until 7:30 a.m. Instead of getting up at 6:00 a.m. It snowed and rained almost all day today and the roof of our barracks leaked something fierce. We just moved our beds from place to place and put raincoats on them to keep them dry. Lots of card playing and sleeping today. Most of us did the latter because we were pretty well tired out. It was too wet to go outside to look around. All we got for breakfast was an orange, a cup of coffee and a piece of bread. The mess is run by Italians and believe me we don't get the eats the American chefs give you. Nothing like we fed the boys up at Issoudun. Then macaroni for dinner and supper, fruit again and a little bit of some kind of meat at each meal (i.e., dinner and supper). To bed at 9:30 p.m.

Monday, February 18th

Weather still very bad and sloppy. No flying so we were allowed to sleep until 7:30 a.m. again. Spent nearly all-day writing letters. We new fellows noticed the scarcity of eats a good deal as we were not yet used to it. We ate chocolate and anything we could find between meals. All drinking and cooking water is brought from Naples. The water here is very bad and also sanitary conditions. The Wops are filthy. We are forbidden to eat in Foggia for fear of disease. To bed again at 9:30 p.m.

Tuesday, February 19th

Didn't get up until 7:30 a.m. again. Still bad weather and no flying. Did more letter writing and some reading today. These wet days gave me a chance to get caught up with my writing and to write long letters home about my trip down here. Also had a chance to talk with friends who had been flying down here for a month and thus learned quite a bit. Of course, we had late dope from France and altogether we had a gabfest something like an old lady's serving circle. Bed at 9:30 p.m. again.

Wednesday, February 20th

Again, no flying and we slept until 7:30 this a.m. Same little breakfast, except that we could buy a cup of hot chocolate, i.e., they called it that, but it was nothing but hot water and cocoa mixed. The grains of cocoa gritted on your teeth. But it was hot and that is something to be thankful for. We all were wishing for some of the Issoudun breakfasts with good hot cakes or fritters, good coffee, oatmeal and milk, good white bread, etc. Today a boy from Princeton Ground school [1]came over to see a couple of us. He is located at South Camp about 2 miles away. He didn't graduate from Ground school until Oct. 20 almost a month after myself but he and the whole class came straight to Italy and started training right away. They had 3 days in Paris on their way over while we had been within 100 miles of Paris for 3 months and never got near it. These fellows had done a lot of flying too and had almost finished their 1st brevet and we hadn't even started yet. We always contended that about 150 of us were the most unlucky cadets in the army. As Sherman said, "War is h---!" and somebody is sure to get the worst of it in the army. This boy told me of lots of training camp, Ground school and college friends who were over at the other camp. Most of them got down here early in November. More letter writing for me today. To bed early again.

Thursday, February 21st

Up at 6 this a.m. Looked like flying weather but after we had gotten breakfast and gone out to the lines the powers that be decided that it was too muddy to make landings. So, we rested another day. Although the last "50" were not allowed to go downtown until they were sure about our vaccination and inoculation for typhoid another boy and myself went anyhow. He is a Harvard fellow from Arizona and a dandy boy. I met him on the boat on our way over and we were on the same cooking force at Issoudun. We also took quite a few walking, riding, and railroad trips up in France without permission. He was in the 1st "50" to come down here and so was allowed to go to town. As for myself, I didn't sign the passbook either on leaving or returning and they didn't know that I was out of camp at all. We went to town by way of south camp and there I saw several college chums and four boys from the same battery as myself at Ft. Myers. One of them bunked right below us. Papa met him, I think. Rowe is the name, and he is from Fredericksburg, Va.

As the fellows had told me Foggia is a dirty place. In fact, it smells pretty bad, and the people are all dark skinned just the class of Italians we have at home. The Italians say that if you draw a line across Italy right south of Rome, everything about that is good and below it very bad. We only stayed in town for a couple of hours. That was plenty. I bought some roasted hazel nuts, some chocolate, and some stationery. The Americans buy up all the chocolate in town on account of the lack of sugar and sweet stuff. We just crave something sweet. Chocolate is very dear over here as in France. A 10-cent cake of Hershey's (not Hershey's but a cake that size) costs 50¢. I have seen fellows buy $25 or $30.00 worth at a time to be sure to have it. Talmone is the best grade here and is Swiss chocolate. Up in France, Tobler's Swiss chocolate was the best. Most of the chocolate over in Europe is coarse and of a poor grade. We got back to camp early and went to bed at 9:30.

Friday, February 22nd

Up at 6:00 a.m. again and out to the lines for flying. We have about 12 lines and from 10 to 18 men or students on each line. When there is flying morning and afternoon every man gets a lesson, but something usually goes wrong with plane or the motor and causes some delay. If we could get a lesson every day we would go solo in about a month. But due to wind, rain, broken machines etc. it takes at least 6 weeks. Seventeen of our crowd were put on a new line. Of course, this was done alphabetically, and I was out of luck as usual. Ern Caldwell (2) was one of the lucky ones. The rest of our crowd had nothing to do so some of us stayed out and watched the flying for a while and then went to the barracks. I did some more writing today. Washington's birthday but no holiday in the army.

Saturday, February 23rd

Up at 6:00 a.m. again and flying. Today all we new fellows were assigned to different lines to observe only. No room for us yet. Mighty tiresome standing around for 3 or 4 hrs. with nothing at all to look forward to. It is bad enough when you expect to get a ride.

They have a flag system here. The flagpole is near the barracks. When the white flag is up there is no flying; the red flag means flying for both dual and single control machines; the green flag means flying for single control or solo men. Very often it is too windy and bumpy to learn anything with an instructor but a student with a little experience can fly by himself. At Issoudun they used a siren to let you know whether there was flying or not. Different systems are used everywhere.

No one on the line I was assigned to could speak Italian or French at all well, so I was dubbed sort of interpreter. I didn't mind for the practice is good for me. The pilot told the motorista or mechanic in Wop and he told me in French, and I tried to translate into English. Some roundabout method, eh what?

There was flying for about 4 hours today.

Sunday, February 24th

Another flying day. It is getting pretty tiresome just staying on the line and not flying at all. Sunday p.m. is a half-holiday if there has been a good deal of flying during the week, but today there was flying in the p.m. due to the fact that there had been very little flying during the week.

Monday, February 25th

Flying today. Nothing out of the ordinary happened.

Tuesday, February 26th

More flying. Rec'd quite a bit of mail today. Package from home with wristlets, helmet, socks and abdominal band and a thin box of cookies from Mary M. Quiston. They were all broken up and most of them scattered through the clothing. What few crumbs were left tasted mighty good to myself and friends. Also got two good letters from my French godmother, some papers from home and some from Virginia (Pearce). All were carefully read. To bed early again.

Wednesday, February 27th

No flying today. Rainy and we slept until 7:00 a.m. Good sergeant who would get up, see how the weather looked and then let us sleep if things looked unfavorable. He assumed the responsibility and ran the chance of getting a good call-down from above. He is sort of hard-boiled and is a rough talker without an awful lot of education, but he has a good heart, and the fellows like him. He was formerly in the national guard and that probably accounts for his rough manner. Got another letter from my godmother. It had gone to south camp by mistake and so was delayed a day or so. I had gotten 3 letters from her, and she had not yet heard from me altho' I wrote to her on the 20th. I felt badly about it for I had promised to write to her during my trip down and had not done it. Every one of her letters contains some pressed flowers. Different colors signify different things. For instance, blue ones signify that one is always remembered; red ones mean deep love, etc. Of course, most of mine are blue.

I went downtown again without permission and without signing the passbook but got away with it. On the way down I took a cold shower—bath at south camp. Usually is hot water but not today. At our camp we have to carry water by the bucketful to even wash our hands and faces with. Seven men are put on the water detail, and they carry it and put it in a small tank. We got a cab back from town and got to bed early.

During the 1st week we were down here, it was mighty cold and wet in our stone barracks and most stayed in bed a good part of the time in order to keep warm. We would get fully dressed and pile on ½ dozen blankets and an overcoat and crawl in. Today, however, we were furnished with small oil stoves which helped a lot, but it is now warm enough to do without. Better late than never, though.

Thursday, February 28th

Up at 6:00 a.m. and flying today. Nothing special happened. Muster today as it was the last day of the month. Of course, inspection goes with muster and that means shaving, shining shoes, and polishing up in general. The roll is called and each man steps forward and answers "here" as his name is called. This is one formation everybody must and wants to attend, for he gets no pay if he is not present.

Friday, March 1st

Another good day. I was getting mighty tired standing around and not getting a ride so I had the motorista ask the pilot if I could go up with him on a "volo di pruova" i.e., on a flight when he was testing the motor. Every instructor does this before taking up any students for lessons and is not allowed to take a passenger along. However, he said that he would take me up on his "V.P." this p.m. So, I was all prepared, but at noon the lieutenant lined up the whole 3rd detachment and picked out 24 of us to form a guard of honor for an Italian general who has charge of all the aviation schools in Italy. Thus, instead of getting a good ride, I had to get all dressed up and we had to stand around waiting for him for 4 hours and then the "old boy" didn't put in an appearance. We were all furnished with Colt Automatics "45" and brand new. We waited until 7 p.m. and then disbanded and got a bite to eat. So, I missed my ride. The pilot was asking for me, the boys said.

Saturday, March 2nd

Flying today and so up early. Inspection today as usual at 1 p.m. both of quarters and of the person. Three days in a row I have had to dress up and that is one thing a man in the army hates to do. When the red flag went up this a.m., I expected to get a ride but due to trouble with the motor the pilot did not get back until late and so had no time to fool away. This afternoon I went out to the line early to wait for him.

Unfortunately, he never got there. He flew out front the hangars and made an attempt to turn into our line but turned too short, lost flying speed and got into a combination side slip and spinning nosedive and crashed to the ground. The machine was busted to smithereens. We use Farman (machine) here. This machine is of the pusher type with the engine behind the pilot. The machine hit 1st on the skids and the tip of one wing and this sort of threw the engine backward. There were only a couple of us handy and we both expected to find that the engine had cut him to pieces, but his head was bobbing around before we got to him. The two of us got him away from the machine, took off his flying coat, unloosened his coat, shirt, etc. and laid him down on his coat as a pillow. He had a 4-in. cut across his forehead and down between his eyes and his one eyelash was cut. If he had worn goggles he would probably have been blinded. His knee and ankle were badly hurt but probably not broken. His face was covered with blood, and he was spitting blood. He was very game and as soon as the two of us got to him he said, "Come sta?" or "How are you?" We said "bene" or "well." The doctor came out soon in a car and we put him in, and they took him to the hospital. Our lieutenant who was in charge of the lines gave us an awful calling down for such a crowd running out. He himself got there after we had done everything we could, and it sure did make us sore after doing our best. He just lost his head completely and ran around asking everyone their names, but he couldn't remember one of them. He was just like a chicken without a head. He was a good flyer, but his stock dropped 100% because of this showing. He said that our running out there was the most disgraceful thing which could happen for the morale of the camp. I presume that he considers it better to let a motor stay on a fellow and kill him if he is not already dead. In this case the gasoline was pouring out of the tank and if it had caught fire, as it often does, the pilot might have burned to death. I had thought that he was a good fellow but some of the boys who had been here longer said that I would decide otherwise, and I did this p.m.

We learned tonight that our pilot's leg was not broken but that his ankle was fractured.

Sunday, March 3rd

Flying this a.m. New instructor on our line, an Italian lieutenant. To kill time while waiting on the line we pitch pennies, read, sleep, etc. There was flying this a.m. from 7 till 11 a.m. At reveille today the lieutenant took back part of what he said yesterday as I thought he would after he had cooled down. He said that it was O.K. for the 1st 10 or 12 men to go to the scene of an accident but that a crowd should not go. And he is right. The pilot, who was hurt, is resting O.K. The doctor sewed up his head.

The Italian pilots were given a "reposo" (rest) this p.m. because we had flown quite a lot during the past week. I took the opportunity to pen several letters.

Monday, March 4th

No flying today. Bad weather. Did some more letter writing this a.m. Rec'd "beaucoup" mail today. Two letters from home, one from Virginia (Pearce) and two from my French friend (Odette). Also, more papers from home and some Princeton Alumni Weeklies, which are immensely appreciated.

Went downtown again this evening. Got a bath at south camp on the way. We went to a vaudeville show where there was music and dancing. Not very good. Girls built like carthorses and couldn't dance at all. Some of the music was good and some of the girls had good voices. Of course we couldn't understand their songs. Four of us had a box. Got back to camp about 11:30 p.m. We are allowed one late pass a week, i.e., until 12 o'clock. The vaccination business has been fixed up and my service record shows that I was both vaccinated and inoculated in the states. About 50 out of 150 fellows have to stay in camp until both these matters have been attended to. So, we can go downtown any day after 4 P.M. when there is no flying, but we have to be back by 9:30 p.m. unless we have a late pass which allows us until 12 p.m.

Tuesday, March 5th

Flying today both a.m. and p.m. 7 to 11 a.m. and 4 to 6:30 p.m. Always too much wind to fly around noon. Another letter from France (Odette) and one from Aunt Annie. To bed early.

Wednesday, March 6th

More flying. Nothing of interest today. A couple of letters from business acquaintances in Maryland. Had sent them cards at Xmas.

Thursday, March 7th

Flying this a.m. None this p.m., too much wind. We all or nearly all of us went to Foggia to-night to an entertainment for the benefit of the Italian Red Cross. Admission is only 2 liras. First of all, the lady president of the Italian Red Cross made a long talk lasting nearly 2 hours. It sure was dry and tiresome for us Americans who did not understand it at all. But after this Albert Spalding, our camp adjutant and one of the best violinists of America played two or three wonderful selections. Also, an Italian soprano sang three pieces in fine fashion. Then to top it all off a regular minstrel show was staged by about a dozen cadets (American.) Paul Nelson (3) '17 from Princeton, former president of Princeton Triangle Club took part. They were really good and played a lot of good old American rag. The Italians looked pleased altho' such antics sort of surprised them. Most Europeans think of Americans as big rough cowboys and such doings would seem to bear out this opinion. The élite of the Foggia were out in full force, but they are few and far between. Six of us occupied a box. The theatre is fairly large and probably seats 2500 and has 4 tiers of boxes. The better class of people sit in the first few rows and in the boxes. 12:30 p.m. before I got to bed.

Friday, March 8th

No flying and sleep until 7:30 this a.m. Rumors of pay day but they turned out to be false. Wrote a couple of letters today.

Saturday, March 9th

Flying as usual. Some of the first "50" are starting to solo and quite a few machines are being damaged, and some broken up. Inspection at 1 p.m. today as usual. We all have to shave at least once a week and that is awfully hard on us, you know.

Little musical this evening. Lt. Spalding played 7 or 8 pieces wonderfully. A string orchestra gave us some fine ragtime and a couple of the boys sang for us. One of our crowd sings in Italian and his class music. The Italians present sure enjoyed his singing. This concert was right here in camp. To bed at 9:30 p.m.

Sunday, March 10th

Up and at it again this a.m. early. Flying until 10:30

a.m. only because we were going to have a baseball game this P.M. with south camp. We all got our glad rags on and about 1:30 pulled out in camious (trucks) for south camp. Before going we were each one given a small white flag with "W" on it meaning West Camp. Some of us were also given megaphones with "W" on them. Lots of enthusiasm, shouting, cheering, etc. The "Wops" didn't know what to make of it. Our captain and commandant (LaGuardia) is a funny little fellow and he was all enthusiasm over the game. In the states he was congressman from N.Y. in the U.S. congress. Suppose he got his commission because he certainly knows no military. But he is a pretty good fellow, and the boys like him. He is probably 38 years old and was born in Naples. So, he is a good man for this camp because he understands the Wops and can get results out of them. He isn't here much because he spends most of his time in Rome, Turin, and Milan making speeches, attending to business, etc. He seems to be in great favor here in Italy. He is a funny fat little fellow and sure does look funny in a uniform. He has a high squeaky voice and talks to us in a fatherly fashion. Now boys don't do this or that, etc. He is learning to be an aviator too but doesn't seem to make much speed. His landings are very poor, and we have a lot of fun at his expense.

Finally, we got started for south camp. In the 1st camion(truck) our adjutant was holding a large Italian flag and beside him an Italian lieutenant carried a large American flag. It seemed good to see such spirit. We stalled a couple of times on the way over and had to get out and push. When we got there, we formed in a column of squads with our Italian band at the head of the column. Some band, I will tell you. They gathered up all the old fossils that could be found and made a band out of them. And they couldn't play much either, but it was a band anyhow and that was more than south camp had. We marched to our side of the field and got settled to watch hostilities. Before the game, a track meet was held, and we won easily. South camp had two famous runners "Windnagle" (4) of Cornell and "Hap" Holden (5) of Yale, and they wanted to bet as much as 5 to 1 on the relay race. We didn't have anyone who was particularly good and so we wouldn't cover any of their money. It was good for them that we didn't for we won in a walk. Their good runner didn't crash though at all. When they were apparently beaten, they still wanted to bet but we didn't want to take their money.

Finally, the game got going. It was a tough scrap, and we were in bad holes several times. We had a very good pitcher, Aldworth (6), formerly with the Philadelphia Athletics and he tightened up in in the pitches. Greenbaum (7), 1911 from Princeton, pitched against us, and he was very good too. They got 3 hits off our pitcher but did not score; the only hit our team got was a homerun and enough to win the game. Only 7 innings were played. The boys at south camp didn't like our victory very well and showed sort of poor sportsmanship. West Camp won 30,000 liras on the game or about $6,000. South camp could not cover all of our money until the last minute when they passed the hat just before the game and covered it all. Our captain had 5,000 liras on the game; our Italian commandant had the same amount; our doctor and other officers here had quite a bit up on the game too. It was our Captain's one ambition to trim south camp at baseball. They are an older camp than us and so feel a little snobbish with respect to us. We brought them down a peg today, however. The two flags were in our truck coming back and we unfurled them as we passed through Foggia. The people seemed greatly pleased to see the two side by side and saluted and cheered.

The class of Foggia was out in full force today. An Italian full-fledged general came over from Naples. Several very nice rigs and pairs of horses. During the game, a Caproni biplane was flying around, and the Italians seemed more interested in it than in the game for they didn't understand the game at all.

Great joy in camp tonight. "Beaucoup" de lira for us. The Captain gave us a little talk at mess and gave the ball to the boy who hit the home run. On it was written "The 50,000-lira homerun."

Today was a mighty big day for me for besides winning 50 liras on the ball game I started in on my career as a flyer. That for which I had waited so long and at times even despaired of ever obtaining, I got today, --- my first flight. Three of us were put on another line with 12 fellows who had been flying for 5 or 6 weeks. The weather was quite bumpy for dual control lessons and so the pilot gave each of us new fellows a "volo di pruovo" or joy ride. All we did was to sit in the front seat and look wise. Each ride lasted 7 minutes. The fellows told him to give us some thrills and he sure did. He "zoomed" several times with each of us. This sensation is much like one experiences on a roller-coaster, only much more so of course because it is much faster in happening. Just before landing he went up quite high and dove pretty steeply and this too gives one quite a sinking sensation. I also got a 7-minute lesson today. Two rides the 1st a.m. is not at all bad. I

Above: Pomilio S.P.3 4658 flew for 26ª Squadriglia, whose marking is visible on the nose, in January 1918. Long obsolete by 1918, these pusher aircraft were eventually relegated to the training units as they were replaced at the front by more modern aircraft.

sat in the front seat and watched what he did and only held the controls lightly. To a beginner the machine seems to go awfully fast and everything on the ground sure does look small. These machines go about 70 miles an hour. The engine is in the rear and sure does seem to make a lot of noise until one gets used to it. A plane has a slight vibration at all times. These planes are Maurice Farman's and ours has a Fiat motor; some of them have Colombo motors and they have a speed of about 90 mi. an hour.

Monday, March 11th

No flying today. Slept until 7:00 a.m. Rain again today. Wrote a couple of letters today. Rec'd one from France (Odette) and one from home too. The pilot who got hurt the day before yesterday is very nervous today. Always after a fall comes a nervous reaction in about 48 hours.

Tuesday, March 12th

Up at 6:00 a.m. and at it early today. I got two lessons again due to fairly bumpy weather which was bad for fellows about ready to go solo. Some of the solo men were furnishing quite a few thrills for us. Nobody hurt as yet however.

Wednesday, March 13th

Flying today. I got my 4th lesson and am beginning to get a little air sense. The pilot speaks French, and I can understand him O.K. He put me in the back seat on my 2nd lesson and I have been there since. He lets me give her the gun, i.e., shut it off and put on the gas or throttle.

Air raid scare this evening. Lights out right after supper. Austrian planes reported at the coast 20 miles distant.

One fellow went solo from our line and did O.K. on his 1st ride.

Thursday, March 14th

No flying and lots of sleep, this a.m. Air raid didn't hit here but the machines passed over here and raided Naples. About 30 killed and 50 injured. Some of the boys went to bed with all their clothes on but I took a chance and undressed as usual. Lots of joking before going to bed as to where we would run and take shelter in case of a raid. No one really took it seriously. Caproni defense planes flying over camp last night and tonight.

These planes were armed with machine guns.

Friday, March 15th

Had my 5th lesson today. The line leader who acted as interpreter went solo today and I was more or less elected to take his place. A very good friend of mine also went solo but broke a wire and was sent back for another lesson. More air raid dope this evening. South camp all lit up to-night for night flying and machines were flying over us when we went to sleep.

Saturday, March 16th

Got my 6th lesson today. The fellow who was sent back for another lesson got it, went solo again and did fine. Letter from France (Odette) and one from Virginia (Pearce) today. More air raid dope and night flying. Two Italians were killed to-night about 10:30 p.m. at south camp. Got into a side slip about 200 ft. off the ground and the machine hit the ground with the engine full on. Machine ground to pieces and both men killed instantly; cut up a lot. The machine was a Pomilio, and the Italians call it "casa di mortal" or "house of death." A dangerous machine.

Sunday, March 17th

No flying today. A guard of honor from here for the funeral of the two men killed last night. Wrote 3 letters today. Received a bundle of papers from Virginia (Pearce). Night flying to-night and another air raid scare.

Monday, March 18th

Got two lessons this a.m. (7 & 8). Have gotten to doing quite a bit of running of the machines now and it is quite interesting. No flying this p.m. We walked to south camp (2 miles) to get paid. We get paid alphabetically as we do everything else in the army, so I had to wait from 2 until 4:30 p.m. Got a bite to eat and went to town. Had a late pass and went to the vaudeville show. Show about as interesting as usual.

Tuesday, March 19th

Got my 9th lesson. Our own pilot was sick. The new one was good, however, and gave me lots of control. Learned a lot from him although he jerked the controls quite a bit. Quite a bit of bad luck today. Several broken wires and two wheels likewise. I got a couple of letters today.

Wednesday, March 20th

Flying today but I didn't get up due to our machine going on the blink a couple of times. Rumors are floating around thick. One is that we are going back to the states to be Caproni instructors after a month's experience on the Italian front. Another has it that we will go straight to America without going to the front. None of us like this idea at all. Men who choose SIA work are being sent to France to train on Brequet bombers. The SIA is not a very stable machine, so it seems. A fellow got into a spinning nosedive today with a SIA but got out of it about 200 ft. off the ground and apparently had control of this machine. But right away he began to settle toward the ground and came down and busted the old bus to pieces. The pilot was not hurt at all. Pretty lucky.

Thursday, March 21st

Flying today and I got my 10th lesson. A substitute pilot today as our instructor is sick. Am helping to make my own landing now and feel that I am learning something whether I am or not. Today marks the end of winter and the beginning of spring. Rec'd another letter from France (Odette) this a.m.

Friday, March 22nd

No flying today. Too windy. Wrote a couple of letters and played some cards. Our old instructor left today. His pupils were doing pretty poorly on the solo line, and they decided they didn't need him any longer. We took up a collection and gave him about 150 liras. We were glad to give that much to get rid of him for as an instructor he was "nix." My 1st 10 lessons did me very little good. One of his pupils broke up a machine today. In making a landing he hit the ground so hard that he bounced 12 or 15 ft. into the air and pancaked flat down and broke up the whole landing gear. One other pilot left along with him. He was fairly poor too. They were sent to Milan to fly at an Italian school.

Saturday, March 23rd

No flying again today. Our good sergeant who used his

Golden Italian Eagle

head and would let us sleep when the weather was bad, has gotten his commission and so is no longer sergeant. He is a 1st lieutenant and is instructing on the line I used to be on and on which the pilot was hurt. The new sergeant gets us up early whether we fly or not. I would like to have an American instructor for he can give a talk to the whole line and explain one's faults. These Wops get all excited and swear at a fellow rather than tell him what he had done wrong so he can try to correct it. A man does some one thing wrong all the time and doesn't know it and these Wops just cuss him out and don't tell him how to correct his fault or faults. They don't take enough interest in telling a person what he does wrong, and they do all they can to stall around and do as little flying as possible. After taking so many up a day they gum up the motor or do something to get a rest. They figure that the longer they stay here the longer they can keep away from the front and that is one place they are deathly afraid of, and they don't deny it at all. Inspection again today as usual at 1 p.m. and we all got cleaned up and shaved. The big German drive started March 21st, two days ago and we get pretty late dope here in the form of official bulletins. Things are looking badly for the allies altho' the Germans are losing a very large number of men. They don't seem to consider the human side of the matter at all but only look for material results in the form of ground gained. We all crowd around the bulletin board and read eagerly every new dispatch. I think every one of us would be only too glad and give up training for a few months just to go up there and get a crack at the Boches (Germans). But the government doesn't see it that way and these Wops act as if they didn't know that they are in a war. At least they don't seem to care what happens in France.

Sunday, March 24th

Too windy for flying today. Did some letter writing and played some cards. I play a little "500" and lots of solitaire. I looked upon this latter game as one for old maids only when I was back home but over here when there is no flying day after day and nothing to do, we are liable to amuse ourselves most anyway. Playing solitaire is descending pretty low for able-bodied men. Received a letter from home and one from Virginia (Pearce) today. Also, a picture of Virginia, which is mighty good and which I appreciate very much. More adverse reports about operations in France. Germans still advancing. Paris was being shelled with a long-range gun which shoots about 75 miles. English aviation appears to be superior to the German. Germans still losing mases of men. Some real hot arguments about the situation as we have nothing else to do. The allies could undoubtedly make the same sort of drive against the Germans if they wanted to waste the men but the people at home would not stand for the sacrifice of human life. The German people have to stand for it. Economic conditions in Germany are very bad and the Kaiser realizes that he must strike now or never. He is fighting vs. time and must do his dirty work before America gets many men in the trenches.

Monday, March 25th

Flying today. Had my 11th lesson with our new instructor. He seems much better than the other one. He gives us more control and lets us make the attempt to do something. Am learning quite a bit about making landings, which is the most difficult part of flying. My lessons now average about 10 minutes, and we make about 4 landings a lesson.

More bad news from France. Things look pretty bad just now. The Germans are being turned back from Paris but are getting dangerously near Armiens, which is British headquarters and a big railroad center. The Germans already have taken the rich coal fields near Cambrai. General Foch has just been named commander-in-chief of all the allied armies. It looks like a good move and should have come long ago.

Tuesday, March 26th

"Troppovento" or too much wind for flying today. Read, played cards and wrote letters all day. Went downtown again tonight and took in the show at the big opera house. Four of us Americans and two Italian pilots occupied a box. I really enjoyed the music and singing quite a bit this time.

Germans still advancing but slowing up quite a bit. They have taken ground about 50 km. in length and 25 deep; the equivalent of 30 miles x 15 miles. Quite a bit of territory. Only 40 miles from Paris at one place now. Casualties among Germans estimated at 300,000 as a minimum. Not bad work for 6 days. The kaiser started this big offensive on March 21st, the Ides of March and the 1st day of spring. This date probably has some significance to the Germans or to the French who are Catholics.

There has been talk of a 3-day vacation for Easter but believe that it is just a rumor.

Wednesday, March 27th

"Troppovento" again today and no flying. Put in the day about as usual. Was quite tired from being in town late last night and so slept quite a bit today. We turned our watches ahead an hour today to save time and we are getting up at 5:30 a.m. new time which is 4:30 a.m. old time. Pretty early I'll say. Pretty soon there will be no going to bed.

Thursday, March 28th

Strong March winds and no flying. Forty fellows from south camp who chose SIA work are to be sent to France for Bréguet work at a camp near Lyons. Thirty were sent up about 1 month ago. Several Princeton fellows in the two bunches.

The adjutant of south camp, a 1st lieutenant was on the list to go up to France. He was a very good pilot and just to put on a few finishing touches took a flight 4or 5 days ago with the best and the most careful SIA a flyer at south camp. When about 200 ft. off the ground they got into a sideslip and the Italian, who saw what was coming, tried to correct for it but the American lieutenant froze on the controls so tightly that the Italian bent them out of shape. After the fall, the Italian said that after he saw the controls were bent, he closed his eyes and waited for the thud. The Italian was in the back seat. The SIA is a very fast machine (130 mi.) an hour and is a tractor with the motor in front. The American had an arm broken, was cut about the face, and had one leg smashed all up. The Italian only had an arm broken. They suffered something awful and raved most of the time. They amputated his (American) leg yesterday and he died this p.m.[2] Tough luck, after fighting off death for 4 days and suffering the way he did. Just a few days before we came down here 3 American lieutenants were killed at south camp in a collision, caused by a heavy fog. They were given a very impressive military funeral at Foggia. Some Italian official delivered a long eulogy over their bodies before burial.

Friday, March 29th

No flying today. We were allowed to sleep until 7:00 a.m. because we were going to the funeral. We got all dressed up and formed at 9 a.m. and walked 2 ½ miles to south camp. There we were joined by another detachment of cadets and a detachment of officers. The hearse was drawn by 4 horses and sure was some hearse. Had a big golden eagle in the rear. Wanted to take a picture of it but didn't get the chance. Six officers acted as pallbearers. The casket was of oak and very nice. It was all covered with flowers. We now set out for Foggia. First was an Italian guard of honor, then the cadets, the hearse and then the officers. Several machines brought up the rear.

We marched 2 miles to town and then 1 ½ miles to the cemetery, making 6 miles altogether. The wind was blowing something fierce. At the cemetery we formed a sort of a large hollow square around the grave. A Y.M.C.A. man from South Camp acted as minister and performed the ceremony at the grave very well. An Italian firing squad of six fired a 3-gun salute and one of our boys blew "taps" at the grave. We were supposed to walk clear back to camp but a good many of us, myself included, grabbed off the 1st cab we could see and rode back to camp. Did nothing special this p.m. Got a letter or two today.

Saturday, March 30th

Five days straight with no flying, so today to break the monotony we flew a bit. Got my 12th lesson. Easter vacation talk was knocked in the head today. Our acting commandant says that we might have gotten away for about 3 days if we had been flying right along, but as we had wasted a week or more, we would have to try to make up for lost time. Our regular commandant, the Captain and N.Y. congressman (LaGuardia), had the misfortune to take a little tumble on his raid and so has been laid up with a slight rupture for a couple of weeks. He left for Rome a couple of days ago to recuperate there. So, a lieutenant is acting as commandant. Have heard that the Captain tried to hold down his position as congressman and as a Captain in the army at the same time but it couldn't be done. He gets some great writeups in the papers at home. I read one that was a peach and was headed, "America's Fighting Congressman." We have a bulletin board in the Y.M.C.A where all sorts of would-be wits are exposed to public view. Somebody wrote up a piece about the Captains raid and shot an awful line about how he drove a Caproni triplane across the Austrian line, swooped down and dropped some bombs, etc. He did land in a camp somewhere in Italy where Austrian prisoners are detained. Guess he would have been pretty sore if he had read this.

Another boy and myself started walking to town tonight expecting a cab, machine or something would pick us up. But no luck and we walked the whole 5 miles. Started at 7:45 p.m. without supper because we flew until about 7:15 p.m. We are not allowed to eat in town but once in a while we steal a march and rent a room in a hotel and eat up there. Have done this several times. If we should get caught, we would get a pretty severe penalty, I guess.

Sunday, March 31st

Easter and no flying. Muster and formal inspection of barracks and persons at 9 a.m. The muster roll was called at inspection and at 2:00 p.m. we signed the payroll. After this we were allowed to go to town. Another boy and myself sent in for a carriage and we left for town about 3 p.m. We spent the afternoon promenading around town, mostly in the park. The elite of the town were out in all their Easter glory and some of them really looked very nice. We went to the theater in the evening. The major from south, a couple of doctors and several other officers raided every hotel and restaurant in town this evening, but we had all been put wise and not a man was caught. The officers were sore at being so completely frustrated. Two of us had a little private place all to ourselves. We got to a barber shop and a woman takes us into her house which connects with the shop and so we are perfectly safe. We had a good dinner at camp today. Beefsteak, mashed potatoes, apple pie, etc. This is the 1st real meal we have had in Italy.

Monday. April 1st

Flying today and I rec'd my 13th lesson. My lessons average about 10 minutes. Today I was the barracks police. Each one of us is given this job from time to time and it is done alphabetically. There are five barracks, and it takes five men a day to do the job. The duties of the barracks police are to have the barracks sweep out for inspection of quarters which comes off every day at 1 p.m. and also to see that the Italians do not get in to steal things. We all like to get on barracks police for we don't have to go out to the lines and wait around for a ride but can stay in the barracks, lie down, write letters or do as we please so we have the place cleaned out by 1 p.m. When our turn comes to fly, we are relieved, and we walk out to the line, fly, and come right back in. All the boys just get up for reveille and go right back to bed. Then later we get up, sweep out and go to the dining room and get some eggs. Well, I was following suit today and trying to ride the "gravy train and so went back to bed. As usual I was unlucky, and this was the day for a self-important lieutenant to be officer of the day. He is the one who showed himself up at the time of the accident a couple of weeks ago. He is sneaky and is always snooping around. He was put in charge of the 1st brevet line but couldn't keep his head and balled the fellows out for little or nothing and so the Italian Captain put him off and made him instructor of one of the lines. He broke up 5 machines in a week and was relieved of that job and sent to Naples on official business just to get rid of him. While away he was put on the list to go to France but unfortunately for us, he didn't get back in time. So, we are still inflicted with his presence.

Well, anyway, he came nebbing around this a.m. about 8 o'clock and caught me in bed. Was not sleeping but he thought that I ought to be up and at it. So, he gave me a good old-fashioned army balling-out and told me what to do and to report to the commandant at 1 p.m. Needless to say, I did my work well the rest of the day and at 1 p.m. was called in on the carpet. Was given a chance to explain but that means nothing in the army for they soak it to you just the same. I was given 25 demerits and permanent water detail. We are allowed 200 demerits and anyone getting that many is in danger of losing his commission. I don't care a bit about the demerits. They are the first thing I have ever gotten in the way of discipline since joining the army and they don't mean a thing in my young life. But the water detail does worry me a bit. Up to the present time seven men were put on the detail each day and it was bad enough then but now there are only four of us and we are on for all time. Two fellows were put on for going away and not signing the payroll; another for being in the barracks when he should have been out on the line; still another committed the same offense as myself. So, we are in for it and start in to-morrow.

This p.m. when I was performing my duties as a faithful barracks police, the ambulance pulled up at the door and they carried in a boy who had gotten into a sideslip at 1,200 ft. and came crashing down without being able to get control of his machine. He didn't remember a thing but talked on aimlessly about whether the machine was broken. He seemed very much worried about the machine. The machine was absolutely pulverized but of course we didn't tell him about it. His wrist was fractured, and his face scratched up a bit. Very lucky, in fact a miracle that he wasn't killed instantly. Luckily, his life belt broke and threw him clear of the machine, so the engine did not land on him. These machines seem pretty safe. They gave him ether and set his arm to-night. Instead of taking him to the hospital at south camp they left him in his own bunk, and he raved and tossed all night and didn't let fellows sleep who had to fly the next day. And this is one game in which a person needs his sleep and his nerves. April Fool Day was sort of a fooler for him and for me too but not so serious for me.

Tuesday, April 2nd

Started in our water carrying job this a.m. We got out of ½ hour's stiff calisthenics anyhow by pumping water when the other boys were called out to take out machines and to take exercise. No flying today. The fellow who was hurt was taken to the hospital today. He is very nervous and broken up and will probably do no more flying. He was always very nervous, and the fellows said that his hands just shook every time he was about to fly. His barometer showed that he sideslipped from 350 meters. He was doing his figure eights and was quite a way from camp when he fell. He was line leader on the same line (line 6) which I am on now. He speaks French and acted as interpreter for the line and so got in sort of good with the pilot. He got in too good with the pilot and he let him go solo before he was ready.

Wednesday, April 3rd

No flying today. Rain. Talk of Secretary of War Baker coming down to visit us. Is in Rome now. German offensive has lost its force, and the infantry seems to be waiting for the artillery to come up. The advance has been too swift for the heavy guns and rainy weather is slowing things up. New water system today. We now use a tank ten times as large as the old one and we have to pump two pumps. It takes us 2 hrs. a day instead of 45 min. as formerly.

Thursday, April 4th

No flying again today. No gasoline. This sort of thing is to be expected of these people. They just kill as much time as possible and in as many ways as possible. They want to keep away from the front until the war is over. We are all fed up on them and would welcome a chance to get back to France. There the people are at least patriotic and ready to fight. If they had used a little foresight, they would have had gasoline here when they needed it. It has to be gotten from Turin.

We pumped more water today. The job is sure getting tiresome. It wouldn't be so bad if we were pumping for our boys alone but we five fellows pump for our 150 cadets, for our officers, for the Italian officers and for two mess halls and the Italians do no pumping for themselves. If the Captain were here, it wouldn't be so, but these upstart lieutenants have pretty big heads with nothing in them. No use trying to reason with them.

Friday, April 5th

"Niente Benzino" meaning no gasoline and so no flying today. Wrote a couple of letters and received one from home, one from France (Odette) and one from Virginia (Pearce). Played some cards today. Also, a little tennis. The boys are playing baseball, tennis, and basketball quite a bit now. More water pumping today. Two men relieved and two others put on for minor offenses. I was put in charge of the detail.

Saturday, April 6th

Gasoline arrived today but not soon enough for us to fly this a.m. We started to fly about 3 p.m. The King of Italy paid us a visit about 5 p.m. but did not stay long. Just passed through and on to south camp. There were three automobiles in the party, and he had about 12 or 15 attendant generals, etc., with him. I didn't get to see him as I was out on the line flying. Had my 14th lesson today. The Italians say that the King is aging fast. I just wish he had dropped in yesterday when we weren't flying on account of lack of gasoline. He might have wakened them up a bit. His visit was unexpected, and we were glad that it was for if we had known it in advance some of us would have been put on a guard of honor and made stand around all day waiting for him. Inspection of quarters and person today as usual at 1 p.m. Fairly rigid today for a change and quite a few boys got demerits for dirty shoes, no hat cords, hats which were not regulations, etc. It seems that they have a lot of demerits to give out this week and they just have to do it some way. Usually, the inspections are a joke compared with those we had at Training Camp and Ground School. With the demerits they gave one fellow today he has a total of 200, but to show you that demerits mean nothing they took off five so they could technically keep him in the school. Allow a fellow to stay in with 200 demerits and they would be no use as punishment. The government has spent too much money on us already to throw us out of the army because of a few demerits. It is regular school-boy stuff. When a fellow gets 199 demerits, they will probably give him 1/10 demerit at a time so as not to have to try and put him out. They couldn't do it on these grounds. This boy had gotten drunk and had been arrested downtown. He was court-martialed and fined 270^{00}, confined to camp for 2 months and given 150 demerits. Pretty severe.

Today was a bad day to be on the water detail because of inspection. Everybody washes and shaves once a week (Sat.) whether they need it or not.

Sunday, April 7th

Flying today. Got my 15th lesson and it was pretty good. We did not fly this p.m. We were paid this evening. Still pumping water. A good many of the boys went downtown tonight but I couldn't see it.

Monday, April 8th

Flying today. We are getting up at 5:15 a.m. now. Formation for reveille at 5:30; breakfast at 5:45 a.m.; formation at hangars at 6:10; about 20 minutes for taking machines out of hangars; formation at 6:30 for calisthenics which last 20 minutes, then to the lines and flying by 7:00 a.m. Here we stay for 3 ½ to 4 ½ hours in the a.m. and watch the flying, taking your turn with the others. Then in the p.m. when we fly, we fly from 3:30 or 4:00 until 7:00. The way the water detail works it is thus. We always have to pump just at time for calisthenics for putting in machines, for cleaning machines, etc. If we had to work, we were determined to get out of as much other work as possible. They do us all the dirt they can so we do what we can to get even. We got two new recruits for the detail today. These boys were in bed when they should have been out taking calisthenics and were pulled out and made to do ½ hour's exercise right before a couple of officers and a bunch of us. Then they were put on water detail besides. We pump the water into a trough and then pump it again to a tank on top of a building. The Wops wash their hands, mess kits, clothes, etc. in the trough then we pump up the water and we wash our teeth with it. Very sanitary indeed. This p.m. when we had a lot of water in it the doctor ordered it all thrown out and the tank cleaned out and of course we did it.

Had my 16th lesson today. Am doing fair enough now and am doing most of the driving of the "apparechio" myself although the instructor makes corrections. Some of our fellows went downtown today to act as guard of honor for an Italian pilot who was killed at North Camp. There are 3 aviation camps and a cavalry camp near Foggia. At South camp there are about 300 Americans; at north camp about 200 Italians; and here at our camp 150 Americans. There are to be 500 Italian brevets given to Americans and no more, so we understand. This is the hardest brevet in the world to get, i.e., you have to do more flying to get it. After passing the 1st and 2nd brevets we are entitled to wear the golden Italian eagle on our uniforms.

Tuesday, April 9th

Flying today and I had my 17th lesson. It was the best I have ever had. Made seven landings almost alone and feel quite satisfied with my progress. Was 1st up this a.m. and so had good calm weather, not a bump. When the 8th man went up a piece broke out of the propeller and the pilot was forced to land in a wheat field. The skids caught in the soft ground and the machine turned completely over. Luckily neither was hurt at all. The front seat and the carlings around it was smashed up, but luckily the pilot was thrown out before the body of the plane struck the ground. The student was hanging head down with his lifebelt still fastened. Rather funny position, eh what? Our line went out this p.m. to bring in the machine. We had to break it all up to handle it and it took us 6 hours to do the job. Three machines were smashed up today, but no one was hurt.

Wednesday, April 10th

No flying today. Too much wind. Played a little tennis and wrote some letters today. Due to distinguished service, I was taken off the water detail today. They caught a couple of poor other fellows doing something and put them on.

Thursday, April 11th

Flying today but our line didn't fly because of the lack of machines. A lot of machines have been busted up lately. We flew this p.m. but my turn to go up did not come around. When we don't fly, we calisthenic for 45 minutes just to have something to do.

Friday, April 12th

Made up for lost time today and had two lessons. Neither was very good. I seem to be in a slump. These come to all of the boys at some time in their course. The instructor seems just a bit nervous or something since his somersault. The weather was very bumpy, and the machine was hard to control this p.m. Had one lesson this a.m. and one this p.m. Got a letter from France (Odette), one from home and some papers from Virginia (Pearce).

Saturday, April 13th

Had my 20th lesson today. Still in a slump and did poorly. A couple more machines busted up today and I had to go out and help bring in one of them. We don't think about the fellow getting hurt or getting off lucky but cuss our luck because we have to go out and pull in the machines. We get sort of hardened to having falls and they don't excite us much anymore. Have had none myself as yet but my time will come when I go solo.

Sunday, April 14th

Received my 21st lesson today. It was in the p.m. and the weather was very rough and bumpy. Am getting sort of disgusted and feel as though I will never fly solo. We are all sort of down in the month on our line. Our instructor is ground-shy or something and makes us pull up or reclaim too soon on the landings. He is not taking any chances on having another machine turn turtle with him. When we don't reclaim soon enough for him, he grabs the controls, jerks them back and the result is a bumpy landing. Got a letter from Grant who is still with Alex. Brown of Balto. Glad to hear from him always because he tells me how things are going at the bank.

Monday, April 15th

Had my 22nd lesson today. Flew again in the p.m. Weather bumpy and I did poorly again. Four machines broke up today. Two dual control and two solo machines. No one was hurt. One fellow on his first solo never got off the ground but turned right around and went clear over; another man on his first solo overshot the line and hit a ditch while taxiing on the ground and turned over. When a fellow does not make good on the 1st solo, he is sent back for more lessons with an instructor.

Tuesday, April 16th

Another solo man turned over today but was not hurt. Got my 23rd lesson this a.m. It rained during my ride and the instructor turned around and laughed and pounded me on the helmet.

Wednesday, April 17th

Had my 24th lesson this p.m. It was pretty windy and bumpy, but I did pretty well. Made 3 very good landings and 4 fair ones. After my 1st landing the instructor turned around and said "multa bene", or very well to me. Got a letter from Mr. Griswold., head of Alex. Brown and Sons and his letter was very nice. Also, rec'd one from Harold Robinson, whom papa and mama met at Princeton. His home is in Newark, N.J. He gave me quite a bit of dope on some of the boys. Wrote home and to France today.

Thursday, April 18th

Flying today but I did not get up. An Italian lieutenant was put on our line today. Our instructor is only a soldier so what the lieutenant says goes. He has been used to flying a hydroplane and was 1st up in this a.m. Guess he imagined that he was landing on water and on his 1st landing broke up the landing gear. We were 2 hours without a machine, then two fellows got up in the new machine and three wires went busted. One hour to fix these. Then another fellow went up and the motor went bad. So, we got 4 men up all a.m. Pretty tough luck. It rained this p.m. and so no flying. We had to put on our overalls and clean and grease machines this p.m. They give us all sorts of yellow jumper suits for such work, and we look like a crowd of convicts. We clean and grease machines about twice a week. This is really work for the Wops, but they are too lazy, and we have to do it. We also built 4 hangars for them which they put off building for so long that our Captain got sore and said we would show them how we do things in the states. And we did open their eyes as to speed.

Friday, April 19th

Threatened rain this a.m. but we flew anyhow. I was 3rd up but our dear little Wop lieutenant had the cheek to ask me to let him go up in my place so he could go away to town. That is the way they always do; ride in the early a.m. when the air is smooth, and they can get a good lesson. And the Americans wait their turn and take a chance on the weather. This a.m. for instance, only six men out of 15 on our line got up but you can bet your bottom dollar that our Wop friend was one of them. Oh, they sure are a courteous lot. And they are professional moochers; go out on parties with you and you pay for everything. Fine sports they are. I spent 125 lira ($25.00) downtown one night when I was down with my pilot, and he paid for nothing at all. My 1st and last time. And the merchants downtown, the cabmen, the kids, our waiters, and all of them are robbers and beggars. Most of our pilots and motorist and officers are from northern Italy, and they are all the same even though they are supposed to be the best class of Italians. No one can get a commission in the Italian army except the rich and the mobility. It costs money to keep up appearances when one is an officer. Their officers strut around in fine clothes and don't want to fight at all. They would rather spend their time in Rome or someplace having a good time. They go around with swords dangling and carry pistols, etc. Fine bunch of tin or chocolate soldiers. None of the boys are very keen about going to the Italian front to fight for these people. Of course there are some exceptions. We have two very good captains here in camp. One of them, Captain Orlando, is of a family which owns about half of the island of Sicily. Orlando is a big name here in Italy. As you know, the present premier is Signor Orlando. And the soldiers have no respect for their officers. They treat them like dogs and the solider is supposed to regard his officer as a sort of mighty potentate or God. Up on the front the non-coms hold back the soldiers' pay in the hope that a man will be killed off and then they can get the money for themselves. Those who have the pull get away on leave all the time and the same poor unfortunates stay on the front all the time. When the Italians were pushed back last fall it was a big sell out by the Italian officers. It was not the fault of the soldiers. Shortly after this fiasco several hundred Italian officers were shot for treason. They were first marched through the streets of their home cities with bands on their arms showing that they had been traitors. The French and English saved the day for the Italians. When we were on our way down here, we passed trainload after trainload of Italian soldiers being shipped to the western front in France. There they will have to fight under French officers.

When you think it over, you cannot blame the Italians so much for whether the allies or the Germans win the war, all will be the same with them. They will still have the same sort of government and will still be kept in ignorance. I believe that it is caused by the Catholic church keeping the people in ignorance and poverty. The pope is on pretty good terms with Austria. The highly intelligent people are looked upon as grafters by the common people and they are about right. Just a short time ago a dozen big bugs in Rome were put in prison for selling a million dollars' worth of gum cotton and a bunch of linen to the Germans. These Wops will do anything for a few dollars. I wouldn't be surprised to see Italy follow Russia's example.

Another example of Italian speed is shown in our water system. We were supposed to have hot and cold running water by Feb. 1st, also a steam laundry and here it is Apr. 20th and we are still pumping water to wash our hands and walking down 2 ½ miles to south camp for a bath. Am not kicking at all but am only stating facts. We send our laundry downtown where we pay 3 prices for it and then run the chance of getting bugs, lice, etc. Several fellows have gotten lice from poorly washed laundry. Many of the fellows have hives caused by too much macaroni and poor food and others have the fleas. I have been troubled a little with hives but am over them now. Sanitary conditions are awful here in southern Italy. There has been some talk of moving the camp to Milan for the summer but guess it is only a rumor.

I had my 25th lesson today and did very well. Am getting out of my slump, I hope. The instructor said, "very good" and told me to do like that always and I would go solo soon. I made 7 good landings by myself in this lesson.

Air raid scare this p.m. about 5 o'clock. The Italians had the anti-aircraft guns ready and also some rockets. An armed Nieuport was sent up, but nothing further happened. Just as usual, we never get to see any fun or excitement. Reported that a Zeppelin was within 20 miles of here but do know anything further. Foggia is all dark tonight, and the people are all scared green and are in their cellars. Awfully scary, these people.

It rained today. Took my lesson in the rain and before we could get the machines in, they got pretty wet. So, we wiped them off before dinner. No flying this p.m. on account of rain.

Saturday, April 20th

No flying today. Rain. They say that we wouldn't have flown anyway due to the lack of gasoline. Another bit of good foresight I am barracks police today. Was taking no chances of getting caught again and so was up and at it early. Bad day to be on this job because it is muddy and then too the inspection is more rigid Saturday than other days. The commandant inspects barracks and men. Got by both O.K. today. Lost my watch yesterday. Left it for a half hour in the washroom, went back to get it, but too late, my love, too late. Suppose some Wop is sporting my watch today.

Wrote to Virginia (Pearce) today. Mail is coming in very slowly now; due to the big offensive I presume. All transportation facilities needed for the movement of troops. We aren't getting much news about the situation in France. The last we heard a couple of days ago was that the Germans had made a new drive near Bethune, further to the north and that they had gained a lot there. A wedge has been driven into the British lines which may force a retirement of all the forces north of this point to save the cutting of the line clear in two. Looks pretty dark. The allies retired south of Oise to straighten out their line. They gave up about 10 mi. 20 mi. and incidentally the Germans are a little nearer Paris. It seems as though the Germans caused the British to concentrate their forces to save Amiens and then launched a monster attack unexpectedly in Flanders (Belgium). It looks as if the kaiser were staking everything on this offensive. If he gains his objectives, well the worst will be yet to come. If not, I look for him to try to get peace. This is about his last chance.

Received a letter today from the tailor who did all my work in Balto. He announced his spring opening and invited me to pay him a visit. Rather behind the times, isn't he? At present I have no need for civilian clothes. Ordered a new uniform and overseas cap from a Rome tailor a couple of weeks ago.

Sunday, April 21st

No flying today. "Nienti Benzino" or no benzine. We had ¾ of an hour of calisthenics as we often have when we don't fly. Wrote a couple of letters today and received one from Grace.

Monday, April 22nd

Still no gasoline and hence no flying except for a few men who were just finishing their 2nd brevets and for 4 or 5 raiders. Walking passes were allowed us for all day but I didn't go away. It was a dandy day. Received my 1st letter from home today addressed direct to Foggia. It came by way of Genoa and took only 22 days to come. Was beginning to get worried about letters sent from here. I wrote home about the 18th of Feb. and didn't get an answer until today, over 2 months later. But all is O.K. now. Mail is coming very slowly, especially that sent by way of France.

Tuesday, April 23rd

No gas and no flying again. We sure are getting sick and tired of lying around doing nothing. These Wops are the most dilatory and the laziest people I have ever seen. It is absolutely disgusting. They put everything off as long as possible so as to keep away from the front. They are scared to death of the Germans.

Another boy and myself got permission to leave camp and be away until 9:30 p.m. We left about 10 a.m., went to Foggia, hired a two horse "carozza" and set out about 12 o'clock for a town 27 miles distant. We bought nuts, oranges, and chocolate to eat because according to medical orders we are not allowed to eat in neighboring towns. We arrived at our destination about 3 p.m. We were arrested, searched, kept in a fortress and the station house for about 6 hrs. Went downtown under guard and got some boiled eggs to eat. Have written home and to Virginia (Pearce) about this trip so won't get into detail here. The town is called Manfredonia and is right on the eastern coast of Italy. Hence it is a 1st line town and very important in the aerial defense of Italy. It is not far across the Adriatic from Austria. Sometime in January an Austrian plane was brought down there and its 3 occupants taken prisoner. Photos of our camp and vicinity were found in their possession. Hence strictness is necessary. We had never been told not to go there so it was not our fault. They sent a telegram to camp and two officers came for us in a car. We finally got home about 12:30 a.m. The officers were not too well pleased but said little.

Wednesday, April 24th

Still no gasoline. At 2 p.m. the two of us who had been arrested were called before the commandant. We expected to get demerits, permanent water detail, confinement to camp, etc. Fortunately for us, however, two of our officers had been arrested at the same town and held for 5 or 6 hrs. the day before we were caught. They were treated just as we were. I think that one of them intervened and put in a word for us. We told the commandant that we were very sorry that we had gotten the camp in bad. He said that if we had told him where we were going, he could have told us that we couldn't go. He said that a complaint had come in from the Italian head of the province and that we wouldn't be allowed to go to any other towns but Foggia. As a matter of fact, the officers caused the complaint by being caught the day before but of course they put the blame on us.

Thursday, April 25th

Still no gas. We are all down in the month and our spirit is getting low. Our camera and the things taken away from us at Manfredonia were returned today. Wrote a couple of letters today and received three from France (Odette) and one from a girlfriend in Trenton, N.J.

A lot of talk about our receiving commissions soon. We have been very unfortunate, indeed. All the fellows who graduated from Ground School at the same time as ourselves, got their commissions not later than Jan.1, 1918. Many men have their commissions now who graduated 6 weeks and 2 mos. after us. We will lose out on the 1st lieutenant'. pay which we should have had from Jan.1st on. That is about \$220.00 per mo. and as cadets we get only \$100.00. Of course, the money part doesn't matter a bit for we are not in this game to make money, but it is just the idea of not getting the same treatment as the boys back in the states. Then too, unless our commissions date back these other fellows will rank us. Another thing to be considered is that the fellows, who came out of Ground School after us, were not training camp men but came from civilian life and so gave up nothing in joining this branch of the service. Most of us gave up commissions in other branches and would probably have been 1st lieutenants long before now. But what is the use of bemoaning one's lot? It looks as if we might stay cadets for life now. A lot of the boys are quitting for this and other reasons.

Friday, April 26th

No gas yet. Card playing today. Got a letter from a club-mate this a.m. and two from France (Odette).

Saturday, April 27th

Still no gas. Inspection at 1 p.m. Rain today.

Sunday, April 28th

No flying this a.m. Still no gas, but it arrived this p.m. New commandant; other one and 5 other officers sent to France for further training. The new one is the lieutenant who caught me and put me on water detail, so things don't look too good for me. None of us like him.

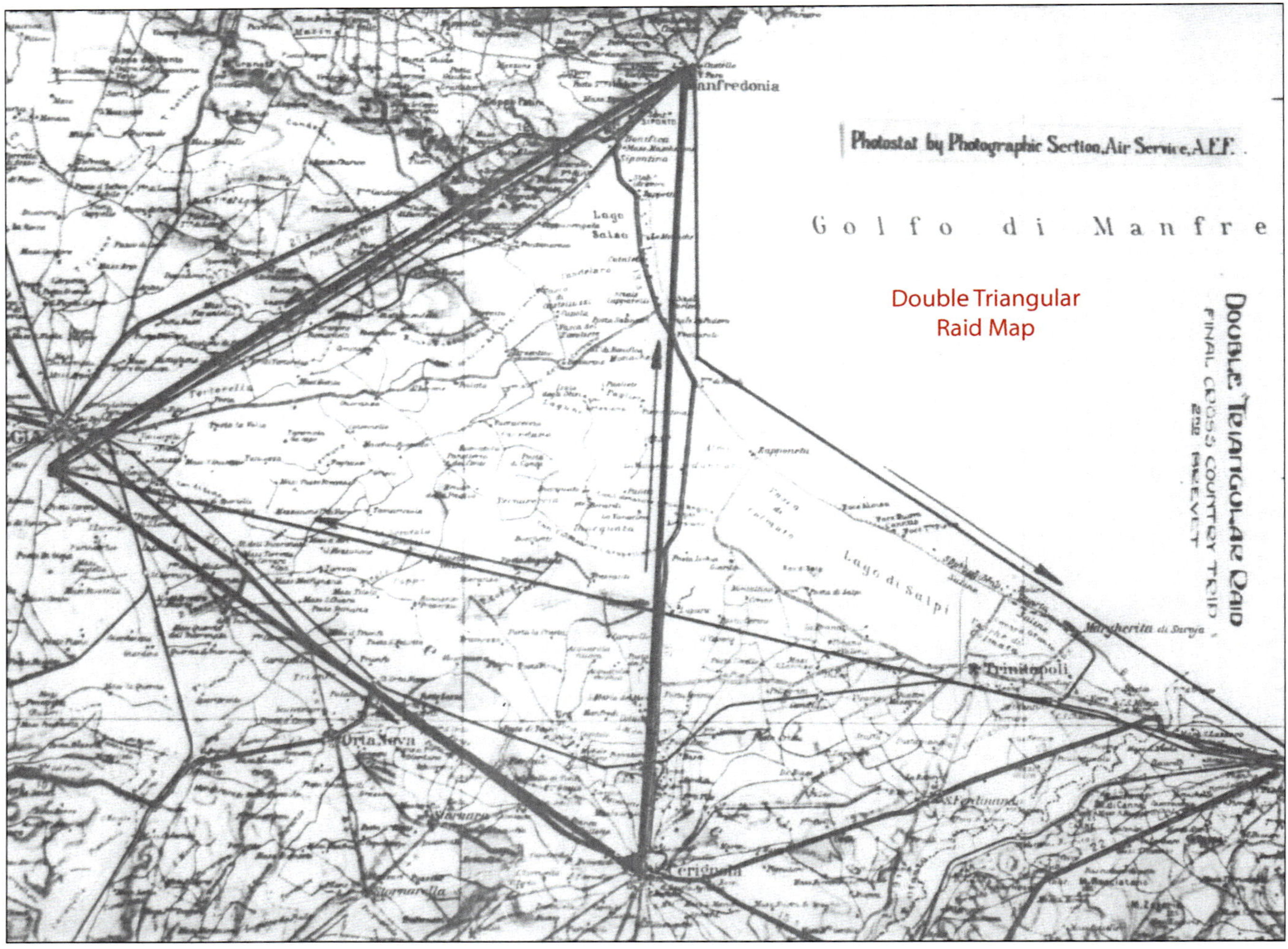

Double Triangular Raid Map

Monday, April 29th

Flying started again today. Our spirits or morale, if you wish, were getting pretty low. As soon as we get flying again our outlook on life changes in an instant. More rumors about commissions but we don't believe anything any longer.

Tuesday, April 30th

No flying today. Muster at 2:00 p.m. after which we signed the payroll. Of course we stood inspection before muster. Reported today that "Hobey" Baker (8) has brought down 4 German planes. Guess he will help put Princeton on the map.

Wednesday, May 1st

Flying today but I didn't get a ride. An Italian lieutenant, who had 17 lessons on a hydroplane and transferred to army aviation, got the 1st ride on our line and I presume thought he was landing on water for he came down pretty hard and broke the landing gear. So, we were forced to lay off for a couple of hours. We were pretty sore about it for these Wop lieutenants think that they are just a little better than we Americans and want to ride first, etc. A good deal of ill feeling exists between us and the Italians. They are a poor bunch. They joke about the Americans being "tests duras" (boneheads) etc. and yet it takes them twice as many lessons to learn to fly and we just fly rings around them. When we stand a plane up on one wing or on its tail, they get awfully nervous and imagine we are going to break our necks. Several Americans have done stunts here that are not supposed to be possible with these planes. We were told that if we got one of these planes (Farman's) into a stall or if we got into a sideslip that we couldn't get out of it and that the wings would crumple up.

However, both of these things have been done several times and nothing has happened. Then too these Wops officers come out to fly all dressed up as if they were going to a fancy-dress ball. Kid gloves, white stock collars, boots or putties all shined up, etc. They make fine tin soldiers. One of them took his 1st solo ride today and was ground shy or something for he made four tours of the camp before he got up the nerve enough to land. He hit the ground once with the motor full on, bounced up and kept going. It is a wonder that he is here to tell the tale. He just got all rattled to pieces and lost his head completely. When he finally did get down a couple of other Italian lieutenants shook hands with him and congratulated him on being alive. One alibi he offered was that his arms were so tired that he couldn't peak over to make a landing. Poor weak little fellow! Another Italian lieutenant tried his 1st solo today and broke up the landing gear. Here are two out of two who fizzle things, while twelve or fifteen Americans will go on their 1st solo ride and never break anything. Oh! Yes, we are "tests duras."

Thursday, May 2nd

Flying again. Caproni flying every night now from 9 p.m. until 4:30 or 5 a.m. South camp is all lit up with searchlights so as to enable the boys to see the landing field. They are hurrying about 30 men thru so as to send them to the Italian front. The Italians are sore because we are getting our preliminary training here in Italy and are then being sent back to France for advanced training and to fight on the French front. But who would want to fight for these people when they don't seem to care whether the Germans win the war or not? But you can't blame them a lot for they really have nothing to fight for. Win or lose, their government will not change, and they will be as downtrodden as ever. I think Catholicism is to blame. The Italians also claim that the U.S. is not living up to its agreement to send a certain portion of supplies to them. They claim that England and France is getting more than their share. The Americans and Italians don't hit it very well.

California boy killed at South camp today during his raid [3]. He was 50 miles from camp when he fell, and no one saw him except some country folk. He fell from 10,000 ft. The engine fell out of the plane and 1st came the engine, then the man, then the wings of the plane. The engine sunk into the ground 2 ½ or 3 ft. The fellow's neck was broken, and he was lying on his face. The raid is 175 miles here while in the states it is only some 30 miles. In the states it is only necessary to go 2,000 ft. or above while here the requirement is 10,000 ft. or above. This is the hardest brevet in the world to pass, so they say. Too bad about this boy for he was just about to finish his brevet as the raid is the last thing and then comes a 7-day leave.

Friday, May 3rd

Flying this a.m. At 12 noon we left camp to attend the funeral. We had to walk to Foggia, a distance of 5 or 5 ½ miles but were allowed to get carriages back to camp after the funeral. A usual military funeral with the rifle salute and "taps" was played over the grave.

An Italian at North Camp had both legs broken today in an accident. Two other accidents at South Camp. Machines were broken into splinters, but no one was hurt at all. We flew this evening after getting back from the funeral.

Saturday, May 4th

Flying today and usual Saturday inspection. Had a small tear in the seam of my trousers and so got 10 more demerits but I should worry. I had lots of company in this respect today. Had my 28th and 29th lessons today and did fairly well. One more good lesson and I will go solo, so the instructor said, but these Italians have a habit of telling a person that and then forgetting about it. A crowd of us call ourselves the "siempre domani" or always to-morrow" meaning that we are always told that we will solo tomorrow, but that tomorrow never comes.

Sunday, May 5th

Had another lesson today but was not allowed to go solo. Don't know why, for I did pretty well, i.e. better than usual. No flying this p.m. Some of the boys are getting cold feet at South Camp due to recent accidents, etc. One fellow started on his raid, came back, and stepped out and said that he was through. Received a couple of letters today and wrote two.

Monday, May 6th

Got my 30th lesson today and although I did rather poorly, I was sent to the solo line. It was too late in the a.m. to send a new man up on his 1st ride. A brand-new man is sent up in the early a.m. or late in the evening when the weather is very good. It was the same story this evening and none of us got up. There were 13 of us on our line and I was the 7th to go solo, just half and half.

Tuesday, May 7th

Took a "Volo di prova" (test flight) this a.m. and made 4 good landings and went over to the solo line. It is a rule here, that before a person's 1st solo ride he must take a ride the same day with an instructor. My 1st solo was very successful. I made a very good take-off and landing and did O.K. in the air. Enjoyed my ride so much that I didn't want to come down so soon. Was forced to drive with one hand for a short time as I had to let out the pressure twice. Was a little nervous before going up of course but once in the air I had all kinds of confidence. Was sitting in a plane waiting to go up when the fellow right ahead of me made an awful get-away. He got going crooked and to save himself pulled off the ground before he had flying speed and just sort of hung in the air for a second. We all thought that he would surely come down and have a bad smash-up, but luckily, he got off O.K. Naturally this did not quiet my nerves at all, but I managed to get away O.K. I felt fine this evening that I had gotten my 1st ride over.

Wednesday, May 8th

Got my 2nd ride today and enjoyed it fine. Everything went O.K. It was rumored today that all of our commissions were at South camp, but the rumors proved to be entirely unfounded.

Thursday, May 9th

Pretty rough weather today and we newer men were not allowed to go up. The older men on the line flew for a while, i.e., until there were two smash-ups and then they decided that it was too rough to fly. One fellow, who had a real bad break-up, lives in Charleroi, Pa. and was quite an athlete at Penn State. He ran into a tree and that is all that saved him. He fell several thousand feet but was not hurt at all.

Friday, May 10th

Good flying weather today. Had 3 good rides. Finished up my giros all except one. Got a letter from home, one from Virginia (Pearce) and one from France (Odette) today. Also wrote a couple. Had not heard from Virginia for about 2 months. Some of her mail was lost, I am sure.

Saturday, May 11th

Regular inspection of barracks today but no personal inspection because it rained most of the day. I took advantage of the lay-off and wrote five letters. It cleared up this p.m. and I got another ride. Am ready for my ¼ turns now.

Sunday, May 12th

Got another ride this a.m. Was not really fit to fly but I hated to miss my turn and so took a chance. I felt weak and was sort of perspiring all the time. Lots of such cases, here in camp at present. I was advised not to fly but did so anyhow. I was foolish I guess for if anything should happen while in the air it might cause a fatal accident. A clear head is absolutely essential in this game. They made me come in to see the doctor after my 1st ride and he gave me medicine and told me to go to bed. I missed two turns at flying as it was, and I sure did hate to miss them. Got to feeling better toward evening.

Monday, May 13th

Last night I took some medicine that the doctor gave me, and I had a good sleep. I think that he gave me something to make me sleep for I have been pretty restless the last few nights. Have been a little nervous and that has put my stomach out of whack. A lot of fellows have the same trouble. It comes from the nervous strain of flying, I think. Quite a few fellows (about 20) are in the hospital with malaria, the fever, jaundice, etc. The medical authorities have condemned these two camps, and I understand we are to go to northern Italy or to France. They can't move us too soon to suit me and all the rest of the fellows. This surely is a hellhole. I had five rides today and did fairly well. I made 5 ¼ turns.

We were paid on May 5th, Sunday this month. It had been rumored, and we had seen it in papers from the states that our pay was to be cut to $75.00 per month. Such things don't worry us much anymore for we are pretty well hardened to anything now. We have been given such a rotten deal all through that nothing would surprise us now. We are surely veteran cadets and as such are a pretty hard lot.

Tuesday, May 14th

Only got one ride today. We broke up a couple of machines. Never a day passes but that we bust up at least two machines on our line alone and a couple more on other lines. Not bad breaks but enough to put the machines out of commission for ½ day or so. One fellow busted up awfully today but had a miraculous escape. Did not get a scratch. Nerves badly shaken up which necessitates a few days' lay-off. He headed right into the ground and with these machines the motor is behind the pilot. It was a miracle that kept it from driving his body into the ground.

Wednesday, May 15th

Flying again today. I only managed to get one ride, however. Our rides last any place from 3 to 8 or sometimes 10 minutes just according to the exercise one is doing I have now had about 6 ½ hours in the air. More rumors about commissions coming, our being sent to France, etc. Have not been feeling very well lately. Not enough sleep, poor eats, hard work.

Well, I celebrated my entrance into the army (Oh! no I mean the anniversary of that occasion) by being placed under arrest. Some of the boys had some trouble with the Wop motorists yesterday evening almost a fight and the commandant called off flying this a.m. because he was afraid that they might file some wires, put an engine on the burn or the like to get even with us. That is just like them because they are awfully treacherous, just like we have around the mines at home. So, to avoid the chance of fatal accidents we were confined to barracks until an investigation could be made and all planes inspected. Nothing was found to have been tampered with and so we flew this p.m. We were told this a.m. that some 300 or 400 Wop soldiers started over to beat us up last night but that something stopped them. There are only 150 of us but we could easily clean them up if they would use fists and not knives, etc. An American can clean up any two Wops in a fair fight.

At a big confab today, our commandant laid the law down to the Italian commandant and officers. I understand that they almost came to blows. Our C.O. told them that we Americans had come down here to eat, sleep and fly and not to clean planes, pull them in and out of the hangars, build their hangars, etc. as we have been doing. He said that the only reason for our doing these things was that we wanted them done so we could get our training faster and that the Wops were too slow and lazy to do them. This trouble will help get us out of here sooner. I think the mechanics are in a position to fix things so that a few of us have fatal falls.

Thursday, May 16th

Only had one ride today. We put two machines out of commission temporarily this a.m. One fellow has broken up four planes in about 20 rides. So far, I have not broken even a wire, but I am knocking on wood right now for no doubt my turn is coming.

Friday, May 17th

Good day for flying and I had 5 good rides. Am getting pretty well along with my 1st brevet now. I have had about 20 rides out of 30. Got a letter from home, two from France (Odette) and one from Virginia (Pearce) today. Am ashamed of myself for not keeping my correspondence up but I am too tired mentally and physically to do it.

Saturday, May 18th

Flying but I did not get a ride at all. Two machines broken up on our line in the 1st hour's flying. A couple on other lines too. Announced this p.m. that no flying until Sunday p.m. or Monday a.m. so as to give time for the motorists to get some planes fixed up.

Regular inspection this p.m. at 1 o'clock. Went downtown this evening to do some shopping. Town appears dirtier than ever. This is my 1st time down in 6 weeks. The place smells bad.

Sunday, May 19th

The powers that be condescended to let us sleep until 5:30 a.m. Think of staying in bed until that late hour. After calisthenics I slept most of the a.m. Took a bath at South Camp this p.m. and then flew 3 times later in the evening. Movies tonight.

Monday, May 20th

Yesterday evening we had a slight collision on the ground. No one was hurt. An Italian lieutenant ran into an American from behind. Then the motor went bad in our 3rd machine. So, this a.m. we had no machines on our line. Then this p.m. just as we were going out to the flying field an awful accident happened. At a height of 3,000 meters or 2 miles we saw a plane fall to pieces, part of a wing floating down detached from the rest of the plane, and the remainder did not look like a plane at all. First the engine came tumbling down and then attached to it by wires all the other parts of the plane in a long string. About 3,000 ft. from the ground the pilot fell out and fell to the ground separately. Of course he was killed, his neck and both legs being broken, and I don't know what else. He surely was a fine boy. I knew him very well in fact bunked right beside him for 2 months while in France. He was a big fellow of about 200 lbs. and quite an athlete. He was a cook on the same force as myself up in France. His home was in Texas. To see a plane fall apart that way does not strengthen our confidence in this type of plane, I'll tell you. This boy was one of the best fliers here except that he would get a little reckless at times. We did not fly any this evening out of respect for him.[4]

Tuesday, May 21st

Flying as usual this a.m. I had 2 good rides. Funeral at 3 p.m. Very impressive ceremony. I was one of the flower carriers. Pretty mean job to walk 2 ½ miles and carry heavy easel on a hot day. I did a little shopping in town this evening. Another unfortunate thing happened this a.m. The steering apparatus, technically called the "cloche" broke off just as a fellow was starting off the ground. It if had happened in the air it would have been certain death undoubtedly. I had been up doing the most difficult exercise on the 1st brevet about an hour before in the same machine. Of course, a miss is as good as a mile but two such cases as we have had the last couple of days tend to make one quite skeptical about flying these machines. One does not know what part may fall off next. The boys who have passed their brevets consider themselves lucky and those of us who have not wish that we had.

Wednesday, May 22nd

Three rides today. Broke my 1st wire today. Was not feeling well this a.m. due to the long walk yesterday, but I didn't want to miss flying. If we had not had bad luck, I would have finished one part of the 1st brevet this evening. Letter from France (Odette) this a.m.

Thursday, May 23rd

Finished up a major part of my 1st brevet early this a.m. It gave me quite a feeling of satisfaction to have gotten somewhere at least. Don't know whether I have mentioned before the fact that we are drilling an hour or an hour and a half every day in the scorching hot sun about 2:30 p.m. They are giving us just as rotten a deal as possible. We drill very poorly naturally and later on in the p.m. we fly very poorly because we are all tired out. Flying is very tiresome anyhow and one needs all the "pep" he has without losing it in a useless way. On non-flying days, a drill would be good for us, but it is too much when we are flying.

Friday, May 24th

Did the 1st part of the 2nd portion of my 1st brevet today. It consisted of going up 300 meters or about 1,000 ft. and then keeping the plane flying at this constant altitude for 20 minutes. This is recorded in ink on a barograph sheet and the record is kept in the headquarters here. It is rather difficult to get a straight and even line as at this low altitude these planes always tend to climb, and it is very tiresome to hold them down. The best way is to throttle the motor down some so that you will not have to push forward on the controls so hard. Then too many bumps in the air make irregularities in the line. The Italians in charge of this part of the brevet said that I had a very good line.

Fifty-seven men, who had completed their course here, were sent to France today for further training. Ern Caldwell (2) was one of them. I surely was sorry to have to part with so many good friends that I had known for five or six months. But such is life in war times. One consolation is that we all expect to follow soon because this camp is to be abandoned on account of sanitary conditions and lack of planes. So, we still have a ray of hope.

Saturday, May 25th

Flying but I didn't get up today. Pretty lonesome around here today since all the boys have left but we are and expect to be kept so busy that we will not have time to get very lonesome.

Regular Saturday inspection today at 2:30 p.m.

Sunday, May 26th

Did my 2nd "eight" today. This time you are supposed to go to 600 meters or 2,000 ft. and keep the plane at this level for 20 minutes. These exercises are called "eights" because the pilot is supposed to fly as though he were describing a figure eight in the air. My line this time was also very good.

This p.m. I did the last part of my 1st brevet which consists of going up 1,000 or 1,200 meters (4,000 ft.) and keeping on the same level for 45 minutes. This gets mighty tiresome. As my altimeter was sort of out of whack and as the air was pretty bumpy, I only got a fair line but plenty good enough to get by.

Monday, May 27th

Got my 1st ride on the 2nd brevet today. It was a real joy ride. All I did was to go up to 800 meters, cut off and come down, doing anything I liked coming down. It sure was real fun.

Tuesday, May 28th

Managed to get a couple of rides today. Got as high as 1,500 meters on one ride, i.e., about 5,000 ft. Did about 3 turns of a spiral for my 1st try. It sure is a lot of fun and is an easy way to get down. One comes down slowly in a spiral; while doing anything else a person is very liable to dive so steeply that it is dangerous and is very injurious to the ears. I have had some trouble with my right ear after a couple of my altitude flights. The chief reason for this is that one forgets to swallow while coming down. While climbing it makes no difference but a too sudden change in pressure while coming is hard on the eardrums. About the best thing to do is to chew gum all the time.

One of the boys had a very bad smash-up this a.m. He got a little too close to the ground while his plane was banked to one side, and he nosed head on into a wheat field. The plane was very bad broken up. I happened to be the 3rd person to reach the scene of the accident. We found him lying face downward and head dug sort of into the ground. He was unconscious but breathing heavily. We took off his helmet, goggles, coat, etc. and helped get him on the stretcher and into the ambulance. No one knew how badly he was hurt. I was to fly a few minutes later and thought that it might affect me, but it didn't at all. Guess my experience helping papa has made me more or less immune to such things. Some of the boys are afraid to go near the scene of an accident for fear that it may break their nerve for flying. I'll tell you this is a funny game with lots of psychology in it.

Wednesday, May 29th

Rain today so no flying. Good chance to rest up which was very welcome to us all. Boy who was hurt yesterday is still unconscious. As far as is known he has a broken collar bone and is suffering from nervous shock. No internal injuries as far as is known.

Thursday, May 30th

Very cloudy today and clouds too low for altitude work. Had two short rides, however. We all attended a short Memorial Day Service at South Camp this a.m. President Wilson's Memorial Day proclamation was read to us and a Y.M.C.A. man made a long prayer. Before the meeting, a list of names was read off to report to the commandant after the service. The reason turned out to be to get our commissions. There was some mistake and nearly all of them were non-flying and so we were not sworn in until it could be fixed up. We were all glad that we had gone over to the meeting altho' we grumbled a lot before we did go. Good Decoration Day surprise.

Friday, May 31st

Signed payroll and mustered today. Too rainy for inspection outside. Too cloudy for high flying today but I got one short flight this a.m.

Saturday, June 1st

Good day. Had two good rides: one to 2,100 meters, (7,500 ft.) the other to 2,600 meters. (8,700 ft.). Regular Saturday inspection and drill.

Sunday, June 2nd

Another good flying day. Took a good ride up to 3,300 meters. (11,000 ft.) Life getting sort of listless, and we look forward only to getting finished up.

Monday, June 3rd

Good weather again. Today I had 3 rides: one to 3,000

meters. and the other two were what we call shots at the square. The idea in the last two cases is to go up to 4,000 ft., cut off the motor and glide or spiral down without putting on the motor at all and then landing in a certain prescribed area marked out on the ground. The purpose of the exercise is to give one practice and confidence in case his motor should go dead altogether, and he should be forced to land in a small plot of ground with perhaps trees, mountains, etc. on all 4 sides of it. When a person has a motor to depend upon it is very easy to put it on and off in case one has misjudged his altitude in landing but with a dead "stick" as we say (dead propeller) a mistake in judging a landing may prove fatal.

We were paid this evening at the rate of 9.12 lira to the dollar. Some board that we owed in Ground School at Princeton was taken out of our pay this month. It was $11.60 in my case. Was glad to get the matter straightened up at last. Do not like to owe anyone anything.

Tuesday, June 4th

Big day today. Early this a.m. made my last flight before going on my cross-country trip. Climbed up to 3,900 meters (13,000 feet) in 40 minutes. Had a very good machine. As soon as I came down, I was told to report to the office to go on my cross country. It is very unusual to do anything more than the "raid" (cross country) on one day because it makes too much flying for one day. Today however there was a shortage of men for the raid and so I was sent right off. Made the trip without incident except right at the start a valve broke on the motor and I had to land without a motor. When anything like that happens to the motor the whole plane shakes and it is dangerous to leave the motor running as it may cause the propellor or some part of the plane to break and cause the machine to get out of control. So, it is always best to cut off the motor altogether. I did this and landed OK right next to the hangars. Lucky that it didn't happen away from the home field as in that case I would have had to make a forced landing somewhere and probably would have smashed up. I followed instructions, however, and was circling the field when the motor went bad. We are always told to circle the field several times and get up to about 3,000 feet before starting off on cross country so as to test the motor. In case there is anything weak about it or it is not running just right it will usually show up after it has run for a little while as it did in this case. I was given another machine and started right out again.

There are 2 legs to the raid down here. The 1st is from Foggia to Manfredonia to Barletta and back to Foggia. Then after a rest at camp one takes the 2nd leg which is from Foggia to Cerignola to Manfredonia to Foggia again. (see map below) I went to 4,700 meters (15,600 feet) on the first leg. Was up above 4,000 meters for 1 ½ hours and it was cold. Was very well wrapped up and all of me that got cold was my hands and face. Once I got up good and high I was able to take my hands off the controls and the plane flew by itself almost of course. I made some corrections with the rudders. The air up high is generally just like glass, so smooth and calm. Near the ground it is often rough and bumpy due to up, down, and cross currents of air caused by different kinds of land, water, etc. On the 1st leg I was out some distance over the Adriatic Ocean right near Manfredonia. Everything surely did look pretty from up so high. Towns, fields of grain, woods, a couple of lakes, railroads, roads, etc. all looked very small but clear and distinct of course this was strange territory for me and was very interesting for that reason. Each town had its distinguishing features; for instance, Cerignola has a large tower right in the center of town; Manfredonia has a pier running out into the ocean. These are the things that a person sees first and remembers. From this altitude I could see the Adriatic Ocean on one side of Italy and the Tyreneanon the other. While that plane flew itself, I beat my hands on the sides of the body and I clapped them around my body and warmed my nose with them, etc. I had two pairs of gloves on, heavy woolen underwear, two pairs of very heavy socks, my own shoes and then a pair of fleeced lined leather ones, fleeced lined leather pants over my own woolen ones, two sweaters, two woolen helmets, a woolen muffler and over all a fur lined teddy bear (a clothed garment lined with fur and shaped like overalls and very warm). Sometimes electric wires run into the sleeves and legs of teddy bears and thus the motor is made to warm the hands and feet. Rather queer way to be dressed but not at all too warm. Got back to camp about 11:15 a.m., about the time it is hottest and bumpiest. There was great change between the air up 3 miles in the air and down near the ground. Every 1,000 feet I came down I could feel a great difference. At intervals I had to use my gasoline pressure pump and to do this one has to control the machine with one hand which I found very difficult. In fact, I found it quite hard to control the bus with both hands. For a time, I wasn't quite sure whether

I would be able to get the thing down OK or not and for the 1st time since I have been flying, I felt the least be scared or as the Wops say I had a little touch of "fifa" (I'm scared). I was glad when I got her safe on the ground again.

I got some lunch and found that I was pretty tired so took a good rest and started out about 4:30 p.m. on the second leg. It was pretty cloudy and threatening rain, but I wanted to get it over with so started out anyhow. The 1st thing, I did was run right into a storm cloud and after getting somewhat wet managed to get through the cloud and into the clear space. Rain feels just like hail on the face and is not at all pleasant. My instructions were to come down in case of rain or in case I lost Foggia because of the clouds. But I wanted to get it over with and so stayed up my full two hours by picking out the clearer spots in the sky and trying to keep Foggia in view. Lost it a few times but managed to pick it up again in a few minutes. When I came down at the end of 2 hours, I found out that the chief Italian pilot had not meant for us to start to in such threatening weather but two of us got away without his knowing it. He did not let the others go.

I sure was tired after it was over. I had spent 5 hours and 14 minutes in the air which is a lot for one day. Out of 500 fellows here not more than five if that many had put in that much time in the air in one day because practically never does a man do more than the raid on one day.

Also received my commission (1st Lieutenant) and was sworn in today. So, I am now a cadet no longer, but a flying "loot." In distinction from an officer of any other branch and from ground hogs (ground officers of the Aviation Section) we call ourselves flying "loots" and not officers for we are not treated as officers but as high school children. The ground hogs who are afraid to go near a plane (i.e., most of them) get all the privileges. Believe me, if I had only known last fall, I would have stuck in the artillery where an officer is an officer. It doesn't feel any different to be an officer from the way I felt as a cadet. We drill just the same, sweep up, make our own beds, push planes in and out of hangars, clean planes, stand reveille, take orders from another 1st lieutenant who is commandant, etc.

Wednesday, June 5th

Still tired today but good chance to sleep with nothing to do and I am sure doing it. Boy from California killed in South Camp today. Took too many chances and fell up against a hangar. Was badly crushed by the motor.[5]

Thursday, June 6th

Not quite rested up yet but doing lots of "bunk fatigue" in the attempt. Mail is arriving pretty regularly both from the states and from France. Awfully hot here now and has been for some time, over 100 in the shade and no shade. Several or rather a good many of the boys have malaria. Promotions are being made to move us over to South Camp.

Had some pictures taken today to send to Rome to geta couple of little booklets showing that I have passed the 1st and 2nd Italians brevets.

Friday, June 7th

Busy packing up today to leave for South Camp. Sixty more men from West and South Camp went to France today. I was the 4th man on the list to be left off, but another bunch will go soon we are told so it doesn't matter. Camp is pretty much deserted tonight.

Saturday, June 8th

Moving day to South Camp. You know the old saying "Sat flit, short sit" and I hope that it is true for I sure do want to get out of this hot, unhealthy hole. Got all located today but do not have nearly as good a bed here as at West Camp. This is a larger camp with better barracks, shower baths, etc. The Y.M.C.A is much better here with a fairly good assortment of books and a canteen where I can buy chocolate, cigarettes (which I use very, very rarely), hot chocolate, little biscuits, etc. Then a couple times a week the "Y" sells ice cream, and it sure does taste good. A couple of ladies (Americans) from Rome are kind enough to stay down here in this dirty place and help make things a little better for us. They have lived in Rome for years. Ice cream was their idea and sometimes they bake enough pies to give us a taste. We have movies about 3 nights a week in one of the hangars.

Sunday, June 9th

This is an awful camp for work of different sorts. We no sooner got over here than we were put on a detail to push Caproni's in and out of hangars. Then there is the gasoline detail, fly swatting detail, barracks detail, etc. A fellow on barracks police has to sweep out the barracks, a person on fly detail swats flies in the mess hall and barracks and one on the gasoline detail has to pump gas into the planes. One Caproni holds 6 barrels of gas and there are a dozen planes here. So, you see that is quite a job. A person on a plane pushing detail has to report at the hangars at 5 a.m. and 8 p.m. to push planes. All these jobs are for enlisted men and not for officers, but we have them to do.

I put in for 7 days leave 4 or 5 days ago but it was disapproved because we were going to move to South Camp. So put in for another today. Other fellows have been getting them right along, but circumstances may keep me out of mine.

Was downtown this evening. Foggia stinks (pardon) worse than ever. It is a rotten hole, and I hope to leave it as soon as possible.

Monday, June 10th

Work today, as usual, only a little more so for we had to clean the planes and to clean a Caproni is just like cleaning a house. It sure is a dirty job. They furnish us with overalls but even at that we get covered with grease and dirt.

We were all given the chance to stay here and fly Caproni's or go to France. I, of course, choose France. I don't mind flying a Caproni, but I sure don't want to stay in this hell hole to do it. If the Caproni school were in France or northern Italy it wouldn't be so bad although I prefer to try a "chasse" (hunting) plane first. Some of the boys signed up for the Caproni training but practically all of them changed their minds after thinking it over and hearing the commandant tell us that we would have a lot of work to do if we stayed here. He said that he had tried to get enlisted men down here to do the work but couldn't. And the Wops are too lazy to do any work. Why some Wop officers, (i.e., they call themselves that) wanted some of the American officers to push planes for them because we were used to work, and they weren't. Guess that you have a vision of us doing it. Oh! I tell you these Wops are one fine lot of soldiers. [6]

Was more that lucky this evening when I found out that I had been given a 3 day leave to Rome. Only 3 days because we are to go to France the latter part of the week. But 3 days will help.

Tuesday, June 11th

Left Foggia at 12 o'clock last night. Impossible to get a sleeper so was rather tired after sitting up all night and only dozing a little. Got to Rome about 10:30 a.m. Stopped at the Palace Hotel, a very nice place. Spent p.m. shopping and driving around seeing the town. I had seen most of the important places and things before, but it was very restful to just lean back in a carriage and drive with nothing on your mind but your hat. It is not at all expensive to hire a carriage or "carozza" and one can ride around for a couple of hours for $1.00 or $1.50. In the evening, I enjoyed a very good meal and took in a sort of Vaudeville show. It was fairly good. There were about fifteen of us up from Foggia but of course we were all split up in town. I travelled with a boy named Austin J. Miller (9) from Elmira, N.Y.

Wednesday, June 12th

Had thought of running up to Florence today but got up too late to catch the train. Got up around 9 a.m. and the train left at 8:15 a.m. Oh! Well, what is a leave for but to get something decent to eat and to get some rest and I am doing both. Believe me it does good to get something good to eat after eating so much spaghetti and macaroni.

This p.m. we took a nice long drive and found a wonderful place in a large park overlooking Rome where one can buy good cold cow's milk, different kinds of ices and biscuit. It is out in a large grove and the best class of people in Rome come there and bring their children to get the milk. It is possible to see the fine Jersey cows right there in the stable. People drive up in their automobiles with their maids, etc. Spent the evening driving around, had a good dinner and went to bed comparatively early.

Thursday, June 13th

Slept until 9:30 a.m., had a good breakfast, did some shopping, and had a good lunch. Met some British officers who were very nice. They are a fine bunch of fellows. Spent a couple of hours out at the park and had some more milk. Went around to the Embassy to find a boy whom I have known at Princeton, but he was not in at the time. He works at the Embassy and when war broke out last year sent for his intended who came over and they were married in Rome last April. After a good dinner left again for Foggia at 8:15 p.m.

Friday, June 14th

Got back to Foggia at 6 a.m. pretty well tired out and found that we were to leave for France at 9 p.m. that evening. Luckily, I was almost all packed up so didn't have much to do in that line, but had to turn in blankets, bed, mattress, flying equipment and all. Also made a trip to West Camp to get my flying book fixed up, turn in some pictures for my brevet book and try to collect a debt of $11.00 or $12.00 from an Italian instructor. Could not do the latter but got a good watch as security for I knew that I would never see the money once I left Italy. After getting all arranged, we pulled out for France at 9:30 p.m. without the least bit of regret on my part.

Saturday, June 15th

Slept on the train last night. There are only 26 of us and we have a private car and private baggage car, so we have it pretty nice. Ours is a large car with eight compartments. Each compartment seats six people regularly and eight with a little crowding. The compartments run crosswise of the cars with doors on both sides of the car, so there are 7 or 8 doors on each side of a car and there are 1st, 2nd, and 3rd class cars. We, being officers, travel 1st class. In a compartment the people sit facing each other, 3 on each side. As there were only 3 of us to a compartment we could rest very comfortably. One fellow could undress and sleep on each side of the compartment and the 3rd on the floor in between. Got my bedding roll out of the baggage car and slept in it and slept fine. Washed my hands and face while the train stopped for a few minutes at a station and grabbed off some war bread sandwiches at another station for breakfast.

About 11 a.m. passed through Bologna. Had a few minutes there. Could get a good idea of the town from the train. Famous University here. Very pretty country we are passing thru; the train runs right along the coast on the shores of the Adriatic. Lots of nice bathing beaches and villas all along the coast. Back in from the coast the country is rather broken with mountains here and there. We passed through Ancona, Modena, and Parma among many smaller places. We were due to land in Turin this evening but had our two cars switched off so we could get up to Milan where we landed about 7:30 p.m. After getting washed and cleaned up we went downtown to a very good Café and had an excellent dinner. There was pretty good music at the Café, and we enjoyed it a lot. After dinner we took a long walk around town and turned in rather early.

Sunday, June 16th

After a good sleep, got up about 9 a.m. and had breakfast. Took a walk out in town to see the sights. Found Milan a very fine city. The people are well dressed and look a good deal like Americans. The town is nice and clean with street cars and all modern conveniences. The Cathedral is a wonderful piece of architecture. The arcade is pretty and in the form of a cross with high class Cafes, movie shows, drink fountains and small shops in it. Ate dinner at one of these Cafes and had a big chicken dinner. Strawberries are in season now and we ate a lot of them in Rome here and whenever we can get them. Paid 75 cents for a dish for them at one place here. All luxuries and dainties are out of sight over here. After dinner I took my turn at guarding the cars from 2 p.m. to 4 p.m. and we left town at 5:30 p.m. Very fine trip to Turin. Several Red Cross trains passed wounded on the way back from the front. Reached Turin about 11 p.m. and put up at a hotel.

Monday, June 17th

Didn't get up until about 10 a.m. Had a little breakfast in bed. Looked over the town until dinnertime. Turin is a good business city and up to date but not very pretty. Had a good dinner and we pulled out of town at 2:30 p.m. Very pretty country now as we are passing through the Alps. It is a bit cooler too. At 5:30 p.m. we reached Modane, a town just on the border between Italy and France. Here is where baggage is examined, and passports are shown. We ate dinner there and a couple of us spent the evening chinning with a good-looking French blonde in one of the Cafes in town. She was quite well educated, and I had a good chance to practice up my French which sounded a good deal better to me than Wop. She had a French Godson, who was an aviator but had been killed. She wanted me to be her Godson, but I told her that I already had a Godmother and that I was sorry. I noticed the difference in spirit between the Wops and the French, even here only a few miles from the border. No more slackers on the sheets. At 9:30 p.m. we pulled out.

Tuesday, June 18th

Slept fine on the floor last night. Washed hands and face at a station but had no chance to get any breakfast. We passed through Chambrey and Aix-Les-Baines during the night and so missed some beautiful mountain scenery. I noticed it was rather cold during the night. Reached Lyons about 11 a.m., went to a hotel, got all cleaned up and had a wonderful lunch. Took a walk out in town to see the sights. Lyons is surely a pretty town of 750,000 and next to Paris in size and importance. The river Rhone runs right through the town and is surely pretty. Saw, in construction, the bridge which is to be named after President Wilson. My friend and I were getting pretty low in funds by this time, in fact I had been keeping him in funds for several days. He tried to get some money thru the head of the Y.M.C.A. there by cashing a check on a home bank but was unable to do so that p.m. We took a good sleep that p.m. and after a good dinner went to a show at the Casino. It was all in French of course but was pretty good. We had a box.

Wednesday, June19th

Slept 'til 9 a.m., got breakfast and went to the station. Pulled out at 11 a.m. Had a very nice trip thru a pretty part of France. Passed through Bourges and Vierzon among other places. At Vierzon, I was only about 10 miles from Reuilly, where my French friend (Odette) lives. Didn't know we would pass that station, or I would have telegraphed her, and she would have come to see me for a few minutes while the train stopped. At any rate we reached Tours about 12:30 at night. It was impossible to find a room in a hotel that time of night, but a couple of us managed to get into a private house.

Thursday, June 20th

Up about 7:30 a.m. and had breakfast. We expected to leave at 12 o'clock for our destination, St. Maxient. Several of us went out to the aviation camp near town to see our friends. I saw a big crowd of fellows I had known in Italy, Issoudun, Ground School, training camp, college etc. Ern Caldwell (2) is here. Good big camp here. Tours is a very pretty town of 200,000. It has good hotels, streetcars and is up to date. Lots of Americans there. Had dinner at the American Officers club and it was the first real American meal I have had since leaving France. White bread, butter, steak, and all. Went out to camp again after dinner and spent the p.m. gossiping. Dd not leave at noon as expected because our baggage car had developed a hot box the day before and we had to drop it off, so now we had to wait for it. Ate supper at camp, went into town, spent a very pleasant evening, and went to bed early.

Friday, June 21st

Up at 8 a.m. and had breakfast at the officers club again. Excellent American style breakfast. Went out to headquarters on business. General headquarters for the A.E.F. are in Tours and there is an awful mob of Americans, especially officers here. Many of them are staff officers who never have and never will smell powder in this war. Our baggage car finally arrived, and we pulled out at 12 o'clock. Slow train, but nice trip to St Maxient. Spent a half of an hour at Poitiers, where one of the 15 decisive battles of the world was fought and had supper there in the station. Arrived safely in St. Max. at 8 p.m. Reported out at camp and because our baggage was not yet in, we were allowed to go downtown to stay. My friend and I stayed at a hotel and got a good night's rest.

Saturday June 22nd

Got up, had breakfast, and reported out to camp at 10 a.m. Our active orders as officers had come and we reported to the Commandant at Foggia by wire. Since this is Saturday there is nothing much to do. The men who have been here for some time go to school and study Army paperwork, Infantry Drill Regs, Army regs and the manual of Court Martial. This is not a flying school, and men are sent here to await openings at flying schools. We do not expect to be here long. We are allowed to eat here or downtown and to sleep here in camp or downtown. What liberty after the way we have been kept in prison as cadets. Am way behind in correspondence and so am making an attempt to get caught up while I haven't much to do here. Wrote two letters this evening, took a good walk and turned in.

Sunday June 23rd

Slept until late this a.m. and got up just in time to get some hot cakes and syrup and sausage. What a change from a cup of coffee, an orange and a couple of eggs. Regular white bread too. The eats are excellent here and we pay $1.00 per day. The quarters are good too, stone barracks. Very nice little town of 5,000 people. Surrounding country is very pretty and the people are fine and hospitable, so different from the dirty Wops. Spent a good deal of today writing letters and getting my final statement and discharge fixed up. Some of the boys went swimming this p.m. but I took a sleep. This evening, I took a nice long walk and went to see some French people whom a friend of mine had told me about. Had quite a chat with the girl and her mother and found out that I remember quite a bit of French. Home and to bed at 11 p.m.

Monday June 24th

Up at 7 a.m. because we new fellows start at school today. First class is at 8 o'clock. 8 – 9 a.m. Army Paperwork. 9 – 10 a.m. Drill; 10 – 11 a.m. Infantry. Drill Regs; 1 – 2 p.m. Manual of Court Martials; 2 – 3 p.m., Army Regs; 3 -4 p.m. exercise or Athletics. We drill with full uniform and Sam Brown belt and it sure is hot work. As for the classes, they are a good deal of a joke because we write letters or do most anything rather than listen to what is going on. I had most of this stuff at training camp, so it is rather uninteresting to me. A couple of Artillery 2nd Lieutenants are our instructors. Rather than exercise this p.m. I took a good sleep and a shower bath. Wrote a couple of letters, took a stroll, and visited the French family again. Good chance to practice up in French.

Tuesday June 25th

Regular routine of school today again. Roll is called twice a day to see if we are all there. Very easy to get out of exercise in the p.m. so I did it again today and took a sleep and a bath instead. Have not been feeling very well for a day or two. It is the change in climate, much cooler up here. The doctors say it is malaria coming out. Several of the boys are in the hospital and it is the same thing at Tours. I feel sort of sore and stiff all over, have a cold and have no ambition. The doctor gave me some medicine today. Took my usual walk and visited the French family again.

Wednesday June 26th

Feeling better today. School as usual. We are all broke and hoping to stay here until we get a little pay. Lots of red tape about getting settled up and getting a discharge to become officers. Turned in a lot of clothes and managed to work my clothing account down to $12.00. Got a good deal more than $12.00 worth of clothes, but if someone loses the bills it is just ones, good luck. It pays to slip it over on the Government. whenever you can because they do it to you whenever they get the chance. For instance, our pay has been cut from $100.00 per month to $75.00 and then again to $36.50 in the last 3 months. We were paid $100.00 for April and May and now have to pay $50.00 of it back and we receive 3 rates of pay for June. June 1 – 14 @ $75.00 per month, June 14 – 21 @ $36.50 per month and June 21 – 30 @ $183.00 per month (officers pay). Then too we have pay coming from last Fall in the States that we will probably never get. And Pershing wanted to take away our flying pay besides. He didn't succeed but it wouldn't make much difference as we haven't received any flying pay as yet anyhow. On the other hand, fellows in the States are getting fine treatment, flying pay even when not flying, getting leaves of absence etc. War sure is H----! And somebody has to get the short end of it. We sure are getting our share of the bad breaks. Then too all promotions are made in the States while the poor devils over here who actually do the fighting either die or will end the war with the same rank they started with. I figure that I lost $800 or $1,000 by coming over here rather than staying in the States last Fall.

Thursday June 27th

More school; getting pretty tiresome and not learning much. The idea is just to kill time until they can send us to flying schools. We must have something to do, and this is what thy chose for us. As fliers we do not handle any men at all, and this stuff will never do us any good. We might be better on leave enjoying ourselves and come back all pepped up for work with better spirit and morale. But that isn't the idea in the A.E.F., especially in the aviation section. There are too many fliers for the machines and the idea is to get rid of us at the least chance. Quite a few boys are waiting to be sent back to the States although they have done nothing to deserve such disgrace. It sems they do all they can to ruin our morale. But "c'est la guerre" (there's war) and we will have to put up with it for a while at least. I would like to get a 7-days leave to go over to see my French friends. But impossible!

Friday June 28th

Still going to school and writing letters. Couple of tennis courts here but I have no shoes and so cannot play. By talking to the French, I find that they think Americans are fine soldiers, much better than the British and the Americans are great pals with the French. The Americans have pep and dash just like the French and that is just what the British do not have. Unified command under Foch is a great thing and should have come long ago. To show the spirit of the French there is an artillery training camp here for Frenchmen who are training to become officers. They work hard all day and then some nights are taken out for night practice. I have seen them coming in at 11 p.m. singing, whistling the "Marseillaise" and having a fine time. Such spirit as this after 4 years of war is wonderful and never can be beaten: and they are fine physical specimens too. The French Army is the greatest in the world today without a doubt and only the Americans have a chance to surpass it. And every man between 19 and 50 is in the military service and what few civilians you see around have an arm or leg off, have been gassed, are partly blind or something. How different from Italy!

They are planning for a joint Franco – American celebration here for the 4th of July and so we were told today that we would be excused from classes if we helped with the singing. Of course, we all volunteered if we couldn't do any more than whistle. The Major in charge is a Princeton man and o we are using an old Princeton football tune with words directed at old Kaiser Bill. It is hard to sing without using the old words.

Saturday June 29th

Practice for 4th of July this a.m. Orders came today for 30 of us to leave for Tours tomorrow night. It isn't hard to pack up for these trips anymore as we don't get time to unpack. Had a good sleep this p.m. and am feeling more like myself again. The friend whom I was in Rome with is in the hospital with the Spanish "flu" but expects to go along anyhow. Lots of people over here have the Spanish "flu" now.

Sunday June 30th

Awaiting transportation to Tours. Were paid this a.m. but after the Government got through taking out its share most of us had very little left. I drew about $30.00 for the month and paid ten out of that for Board. So, I have some $20.00 to last me a month. Have $45.00 mileage money coming for my trip up from Italy but the Government. is mighty slow about paying such things. Put in a claim for it over a week ago and it only goes to Tours 7 hours distant.

Fine meal this noon. Chicken, potatoes, peas, asparagus, pie etc. They sure feed us fine here for being in the Army, the best I have found on this side. After bidding good-bye to several French friends, we left at 8 p.m. for Tours. Stopped overnight at Poitiers, got in there about 11 p.m.

Monday July 1st

Up and caught the train for Tours at 9 a.m. arriving at Tours about noon. Had dinner at the Y.M.C.A. where they give you a good old American dinner all served together on one plate for 3 francs (50 cents). Went out to camp along with baggage in the p.m. Got settled in before night. Food very good but the barracks were not so comfortable. Beds like we had in Issoudun made by stretching burlap over two by fours. Four beds are built all together and when one fellow crawls in and he disturbs the other three. Then too they are not comfortable as a person sleeps with head and feet up while the beds sag badly in the middle. One can put up with these things to be back in France, however.

The Major in charge of flying here called us all into his office this evening and gave us a talking to. His name is Davidson, and he used to be Commandant of Cornell Ground School. Last winter he was supposed to be a good friend of the cadets but now he is just the reverse. In one of his talks to a bunch of cadets, who had just been commissioned officers, he told them that they were a crowd of nuisances and that the Government. could win the war better without them and made other such insulting remarks. One fellow was wise enough to take it all down in shorthand and the Major was severely reprimanded from above. This incident, a little trouble with a French girl and several things are tending to getting him in pretty bad. He told us that the 1st crowd of fellows who came up from Italy had blown around how much they knew about flying, etc. and got the instructors sore and broke up a lot of planes and got in "Dutch" in general. Naturally, they had gotten a poor opinion of men trained in Italy and so all of us had to suffer more or less. He told us to unlearn as quickly as possible what we had learned in Italy and to teach his instructors just as little about flying as possible. Pretty sarcastic! Ten of our crowd were lucky enough to be sent on to an English flying school at Vendome, about 25 miles away. The English treat their flyers just as nice as the Americans do rotten.

Tuesday, July 2nd

Had flying equipment issued us this a.m. and were put on the flying list. Got a good joy ride this a.m. These are funny boats; look just like a bathtub with a man in the back end. In Italy we flew planes with the propellor in the back of the pilot (pusher), these planes up here are tractors with the propellor in the front. These are smaller and control with a stick which comes up between one's legs, while the plane that we flew in Italy control like an automobile. These are quite different to fly, and one has to pay close attention to these differences, or he may get into something he may not get out of. The landing too is much different.

We sure do get up early in the a.m. (3:45 a.m.) when it is still dark, and the sergeants take roll call with lanterns. Out on flying field at 4:45 a.m., flying until 10 a.m., drill and calisthenics from 10:30 to 11:30 a.m. in the hot sun, lunch at 12 and then a sleep until 3 p.m. Flying again from 4:30 p.m. to 9:30 p.m. Only from 10:30 p.m. to 3:45 am. sleep at night. Not enough! Had a second lesson this evening and did O.K.

Wednesday, July 3rd

Good flying weather again today. Had one 15-minute ride. Weather better up here than Italy for flying. Not so bumpy and it is possible to fly later in the afternoon. This is because it is not nearly so hot up here and then one doesn't have the cross currents of sea breezes to deal with. We are flying Caudrons here and they don't have ailerons but the whole wing must be warped to control the bus. It is very difficult to handle these planes in the wind and bumps. This is a large school here and they have many types of planes. For instance: Breguet's, Nieuports (3 types), Sansom's, Caudrons, Sopwith Camels, A.R.'s, DeHavilland 45 with Liberty motors. Then planes drop in from other schools (British and American). Some of these are: Avro, Sop pupa, Bristol scouts, La Tour, and others. There is also a big observers school here to train men for artillery observation: also, a Radio School. Have seen any number of old friends here from college, ground school, training camp, Issoudun, Italy and all over.

Thursday, July 4th

Holiday for one day only at this camp but it was a relieve not to hear the old sirens blow out at 3:45 a.m. and hear the sergeants yell "Hit the deck!" So, I had a good sleep until 10 a.m. A squadron of 16 British planes came over from Vendome, a nearby school and did all sorts of stunts. Fly over camp and then over the town of Tours. It was worse than a 3-ring circus and was impossible to watch all of the planes at once. It is interesting to watch one plane do loops, side slips, spirals, dives, vrilles, etc. but it is really exciting to watch 16 of them doing them all at one time. Some of the planes flew American flags in our honor. After a fine exhibition they all landed in our field and took dinner at our camp.

There was quite a celebration at Tours and in fact all over France in honor of the 4th. In Tours there was a baseball game and big track meet in the a.m. and p.m. and some sort of big celebration at one of the theaters in honor of the Americans. Then too there was a big dance at the Officer's Club and several others at different places in town. I went out to camp rather early for I had to get up and fly at 3:45 the next morning and carousing all night does not give one a very clean head. At Issoudun they were given 4 days off (Thursday, Friday, Saturday, and Sunday). My French friend (Odette) wanted me to come over to see her but with only one day off it was impossible. Wish I had been at Issoudun for the 4th.

It came out in the French, English, and American papers today that there were one million Americans in France, that 125 ships were launched in America today, that Paris and many other French cities were renaming streets, Squares, bridges, etc. for President Wilson. England is also celebrating the 4th. It sure makes a person feel proud to be an American and we hear compliments for America and Americans on all sides. Ther French can't give enough praise.

Friday, July 5th

Pretty hard to get back to work this a.m. Everybody more or less dead. Had two lessons this a.m. but was too tired to get much out of them. Learned this a.m. that a fellow (10-Carl Kohlmayer) I had known slightly at Princeton ground school was killed yesterday. He and two other fellows, also from Princeton Ground School, took up 3 planes and flew over the park where the ballgame and track meet were going on. He tried to loop too close to the ground and ran the plane right into the ground. He was instantly killed and the fellow with him was injured. I had seen this boy downtown at 3 p.m. and at 5:30 p.m. he was dead. It was all for a little fun too as they had not been ordered to fly at all. It pays only to fly on duty, otherwise it is too great a risk for oneself and for the government.[7]

Saturday, July 6th

Excellent flying weather and I had a good flying lesson this a.m. Very hard to get up at 3.45 a.m. and eat breakfast in the dark i.e. I mean by electric light. Usually breakfast is coffee, oatmeal, and doughnuts with French toast sometimes instead. Good breakfast but a person gets pretty hungry before noon. Am usually hungriest about drill time. Lunch is a good meal with meat, potatoes and peas or asparagus or the like. Also, lemonade and pie. Pie sure does go good. The evening meal is light and comes at 5 p.m. If we have meat at all in the evening it is cold meat and salad and greens. Then after flying at about 9:30 a.m. the cooks sell egg sandwiches, and a person is usually hungry enough to eat.

Sunday July 7th

No flying today. Up here we fly harder during the week and take Sunday off. In Italy it was fly every day. Had a good sleep this a.m. Inspection of quarters by the Major at 10.00 a.m. Good chicken dinner. Went downtown late in the p.m. and had supper down there and came back to camp around 9:30 p.m.

Monday July 8th

Had a good lesson today. Am getting the hang of landing this bus better. Kohlmeier is the name of the boy who was killed on the 4th. The government furnishes a certain amount for a box, but the friends of the boy usually like to buy something a little better. At times, these burial funds are a little shy and today a couple of fellows who had failed to sign the passbook when they came back from town were given their choice between a week's confinement to camp, or a voluntary contribution to the "coffin" fund. Pretty mean idea I think but is in keeping with the manner in which we are treated at this camp. We are treated just like schoolboys and not at all like officers. We have to sign a book at 9:30 at night to show that we are in camp. We are put on our honor that we sign the book ourselves and we will not get someone else to do it. They put us on our own honor and at the same time count our words of honor as officers as much, so we just treat the matter accordingly. Then too they are mighty mean about granting passes to town so at times we go down regardless. They don't seem to meet us halfway at all in the Aviation Service. It is just the opposite with the French and British and perhaps the American policy will change after lots of pilots are killed off and new ones are not so plentiful as at present. Pilots are a drug on the market now.

Tuesday July 9th

Had a fine lesson today and ought to go solo soon. There are lots of minor accidents here, resulting in a few broken bones and bruises and sometimes nothing at all. One day recently 19 machines were busted up with no one hurt. The motors in these Caudron are very old and often go bad and cause forced landings in wheatfields, etc. A forced landing in a wheat field means a turnover invariably, but usually no damage to the pilot. One fellow was killed this evening in a Nieuport some distance from camp. I didn't know him.

Wednesday July 10th

No flying today. Rain. Good sleep this a.m. Wrote several letters today. Received a box of cakes and candy from my Reuilly friend (Odette). She is always begging me to come to spend a weekend with them, but I can't get away from this place long enough.

Thursday July 11th

Good weather again today and I had a very good lesson. Made 3 excellent landings. The instructor told me so, but for some reason none of us were sent solo. Noticed 3 Farman planes here today, also a Voisin. The latter has 4 wheels just like an automobile and really has brakes on the rear set. The boys claim that every time a person goes up in a Farman or a "Jay Cat" he gets killed. A "Jay Cat" is a bi-motored Caudron. Several fellows have been killed here in them and two fellows were killed in a Farman right over the hangars. The one boy was a clubmate ad classmate of mine and I knew him very well. His name was J. N. Dowell (11) of Wash., D.C., and he sure was a fine fellow with a sterling character. I used to see him at Issoudun almost every day last winter. He was Captain of the Princeton Cross Country team his senior year. Two other boys were killed the other day in a Caudron. A puff of wind caught them under one wing when they were making a turn, and they were turned over on their back and came down that way. Compared with Issoudun there are not many fatal accidents here at Tours. For a couple of months this Spring they killed on average 5 a week. It runs in streaks that way and there haven't been so many lately.

Friday July 12th

Did not get a flight today. Motor didn't work well this a.m., and it was too windy to fly this evening. Am confined to camp for a period of 3 days for being in the kitchen for a drink of water when I should have been on my way to the flying field. Just another example of the way they treat flying Lieutenant's. We are just like children to them. Inspector General here today and we put on all our best togs to stand inspection. Although it rained, we had to stand out and take it without saying a thing and our best uniforms looked rather sorry. The inspection was to catch fellows with fellows pockets, split tails in their coats, hooks for Sam Brown belts, high laced boots, etc. No names were taken but we were all warned. Men who had complaints about the way they were being treated where given a chance to state their cases in writing. The Inspector got quite an earful from fellows who had been kicked off flying or "radiated" for some trivial little thing. And in some cases, it did good and some of the boys were reinstated. He also called some fellows in to find out about the treatment we were getting around camp and the morale and spirit of the Air Service in general. And again, got an earful.

Saturday July 13th

Three lessons today but I don't seem as good as yesterday. Our instructor had an accident this evening. He tried to take off the ground in too short a distance. I had just finished my lesson, and another fellow was ready for his 2nd ride. We were taking off over a road, trees, and telephone wires. He was feeling fine this evening and whenever I took off, he would make me stay low and head for the trees and wires and then just as we would get about to them, zoom up over them. This time he zoomed almost with the nose straight up in the air but couldn't clear the wires, two of which (one live) he broke and took parts of the treetops along. Everyone looked for them to come down on their back, but they managed to get squared up and it looked as if they were going to get away O.K. But all at once they went into a side slip and crashed into a wheat field. Neither one was hurt to speak of although they both had several little cuts and bruises. The machine was an awful wreck.

Sunday July 14th

Another day off. Good sleep and inspection at 10:00 a.m. Chicken for dinner. Ice cream and cake for supper. Not bad for the Army. Went to town for a little while this evening after supper. Lots of people. Today is the French 4th of July.

Monday July 15th

Getting awfully tiresome getting up so early. A fellow can't keep it up long. It is too hot to sleep much during the day. But we hear that it is 124 in the shade in Foggia. Some hot, eh?

Well, I had my turn to be in a smash up today. Went up on my 1st ride with the same instructor who had fallen on Saturday. We were going along nicely. I had taken off and had flown quite a while in the air when I saw him shake his head, cut off the motor and grab the controls. I didn't know what he wanted to do. Thought perhaps he wanted to fool around and do some stunts or that he noticed the motor going real badly and was going to make a forced landing. So, I let him have the controls, but quick as a flash the plane was standing up vertically on one wing and going for the ground. I was more or less fascinated by watching the ground come up at us and I didn't look in his direction at all. I figured that he knew what he was doing and that he had 150 hours flying in a Caudron to my 3 hours. And that if I tried to do anything I might just be hindering him. So, I trusted him to bring it out right up until we crashed. We fell about 450 – 500 feet and ended up in a vineyard up against a small tree. The vines were about 2½ or 3 feet high with a stake at each vine. Nasty place to fall. The nose of the plane and the one wing hit about the same time. The belt in the rear seat is very strong and unless the fall is very hard doesn't break. But it broke with me, and I found myself out among wing struts and wires. He yelled to see if I was hurt, I tried to answer but couldn't. It felt as if something had run into my stomach; but it hadn't, and I only had the wind knocked out of me by the force of the fall. At last, we both got ourselves untangled and out of the wreckage. I was all bent double but soon got my wind. He had a bad blow behind one ear, his right shoulder was like a piece of raw meat, his back and legs were cut and bruised, and he had a cut on his nose. I was cut a little and bruised about the legs, arms, and chest. He couldn't remember a thing that had happened, didn't even remember starting off the ground. I remembered everything well and told him just what had happened. The ambulance came up soon and took us back to camp. During the ride and while the doctor was fixing us up, he asked me fully 15 times what had happened. I got tired telling him and the doctor finally told him to keep quiet. His mind was out of whack, and he didn't even remember that he had fallen on Saturday. He seemed to think that he had passed out or fainted in the air and I guess that is what happened. If I had thought that anything like that had happened, I sure would have tried to do my best to have kept the machine from falling. But I thought all the time he was fighting to save the fall. It seems that no one was flying the thing and naturally we came down. Another instructor in another plane above and behind us said that it looked as if Schultz (from Columbus, Ohio.) had passed out and was lying down over the controls. He was bustled off to the hospital in Tours while I was allowed to stay at camp.

Just after I had fallen, I felt that I could take any plane up and fall any distance and not get hurt at all. I was chock full of confidence. Now I understand the psychology of sending a man up at once in another plane if he is not badly hurt. The English do it and the Americans do sometimes.

Tuesday July 16th

Feeling awful sore and stiff today. My right arm and right leg stiffened up and collar bone and stomach pretty sore. Am sore under the chin; guess something hit me there. Did not go out and fly or drill this a.m. Doctor excused me from all formations for a few days. Don't want to get behind my crowd so went out and flew this evening. Our other instructor took me out as a passenger, flew over Tours and did vrilles spirals, side slips, renversements and all the stunts to give me confidence again. He advised me to rest up for a few days, but I said not. Just as I was all confidence last night, I was the opposite this a.m. and got worse as the day passed. But feel better after the ride. The sooner one gets a flight after a fall the better.

Wednesday, July 17th

Still feeling bum but flew anyhow and had a fair lesson. Lots of fellows leaving here for Issoudun and others coming from Issoudun and other camps. Some fellows who wanted Caproni work and even started to fly them were taken off and sent up here. Rumored that the school at Foggia is to be closed up. Too slow work to train under the Italians.

Thursday, July 18th

Rain and no flying today. Just as glad as it gives me a chance to rest up a bit. Have black and blue places all over me and my stomach is pretty sore. Hear that Schultz is a good deal better and wants to talk to me, but I don't feel well enough to go downtown.

Friday, July 19th

Feeling punk this a.m. but flew anyway and did OK. Was sent solo made 3 flights and was lached or turned loose from dual control. Thought that I might have lost some of my confidence but did not feel that way when I flew alone. It is always nice without an instructor. Was called to the office to make a report on the machine we broke. Told them what I knew about it and that was all there was to it. A report has to be sent into headquarters on each machine busted. When an instructor is along, he is responsible for the plane. So, I have nothing to worry about along that line. If I had been alone, I probably would have been radiated and not have been allowed to fly anymore. So far in my training I have not even broken a wire or a landing gear, i.e., when I was doing the flying and was alone. But my turn will come no doubt.

Saturday, July 20th

Did not succeed in finding the flying field this a.m. so came back and landed and went in and went to bed. The field is some 5 miles from camp and the fellow in charge rides out in an automobile while he has some of the students fly the planes out. I did my best to find the place but like lots of others failed and came back when my motor started to miss. Had good ride for ½ hour though. No flying this evening because of too much wind.

Sunday, July 21st

Another day off. Good sleep and good dinner. Ice cream for supper. Hung around camp and wrote letters all p.m. and took a short walk in the evening. In the p.m. and evening when the weather is nice there is always a big crowd of people walking, driving, and riding bicycles out past the camp. They like to see the flying of which there is very little on Sunday. Other evenings a good many people are out watching the planes, Everybody, old and young, male, and female ride bicycles over here. It is their favorite form of exercise.

Monday, July 22nd

This a.m. I went out to the truck to the solo field to make sure of getting there. Two other fellows flew planes out, one of them saying that he knew exactly where the field was. The instructor, another fellow and myself waited and waited for them to come out. Finally, they came, flew over and around us time and time but couldn't see us to save themselves. It sure did look comical to see them for it looked easy to us for them to find the plane. But the instructor said that I had done the same thing on Saturday. The fellows gave up looking for us and went back to camp and so did we. Since we all spent time in hunting the field we were lached or turned loose from that field. We would only have had 3 short flights to make anyway so it didn't matter.

This evening, I went to another solo field, made five short flights, flew a machine back to the hangars and I was through with the course here at Tours. Not much of a course but the school was about to be closed up for pilots and made into a school of observation. So, we get no acrobatics as formerly and it is just a matter of form to put a man through. It is our loss as we need all the flying experience we can get before going to the front. They don't do things in such a slip shot manner in the schools in the states. Very bumpy this evening and it sure kept me busy juggling the controls.

Tuesday, July 23rd

Quite a relief to be all through and not have to get up to fly. One has to stand reveille anyhow at 3:45 a.m. but can go right back to bed. Fortunately for me the sergeant has not put me on the roll since I fell so I don't have to get up or to drill or anything. Went to town without a pass as usual this evening.

Wednesday, Jul 24th

Do not get up until 9 or 9:30 a.m. now. Nice to lie in bed when others have to get up in the middle of the night. Have a great time writing letters and playing solitaire to pass away the time. Went downtown again this evening to do a little shopping. Am having a pair of full-dress boots made. They will cost between $40 and $45. Pretty high but all things are that way over here.

Thursday, Jul 25th

Same old thing today. It is beginning to get monotonous with nothing to do and all day to do it. Was at the "Y" last night. Fairly good movies and some queer Chinese acting. Believe me it is funny to hear them sing. They pull some stunts with swords and do pantomime fighting. When they sing, they jabber and beat on a saucer or plate with chopsticks. There are hundreds of them around here doing the dirty work. They take the place of German prisoners at this camp.

Friday, July 26th

Letter writing and solitaire. Took a long walk this evening with a boy by the name of Lancaster (12). He is from Virginia and was one of my roommates at Ground School. Two other roommates from Ground School are here too; one has quit flying (never wanted to fly I believe) and is a ground officer and the other is radiated because he smashed up a couple of planes. He is trying to get a transfer but if he can't, he will probably be sent back to the states and will lose his commission. Many fellows I know of have been treated that way. It isn't right for if a fellow can't fly, it isn't his fault. The state put the cart before the horse, send a man to Ground School and spend a lot of money before they even know whether a fellow can ride in a plane with somebody driving it. It would be much more logical to test a man out and see if he can fly before sending him to school. It would save money and be better for the fellow himself. With us we were sent over here and have done our best and now those who can't fly are sent back home more or less in disgrace and to lose their commissions. Only about 50% of the men finishing Ground School make good fliers. Most of the boys have the ability and would make good in another branch of the service if given the chance but very little chance is given them over here and most of them turned down commissions at training camp and now, they go back to be drafted while men of far less ability are getting commissions every day. It doesn't look right but it is the truth.

Saturday, July 27th

Getting very monotonous this life. Expected to be sent to Issoudun before this but orders came the other day that it was full and to send no more men until further orders. St. Maixent is the same, so we are here for a while. Up to the present they have been allowing the boys 3 days to make a half day trip so that they can have a little vacation and go to Paris. But even that is to be discontinued. Several of us have asked for 7 days leave but all except a very favored few have failed.

Took a walk this evening and met an old farmer who made us go home with him and have some wine and meet the family. I tell you the French are surely hospitable, and they sure do like the Americans. They are just full of praise for what our boys are doing on the front. This is the richest part of France agriculturally speaking and it sure is pretty now especially from an aero plane. As far as the eye can carry there are fields and fields of wheat and oats. It sort of makes me homesick at times. All along here is the valley of the Loire and it is exceedingly fertile, and its banks are dotted with beautiful chateaux and quaint little villages.

Sunday July 28th

Inspection at 10 a.m. Chicken dinner. Went downtown this p.m. and tried to have a game of golf or tennis at the golf club but could not get a hold of a pair of tennis shoes. The club is French, but they have given American officers privileges of the club for a small fee.

Monday, July 29th

Devote most of my time to playing solitaire and reading news of the great drive the allies are making near Soissons and Rheines. It sure is a master stroke and well directed and looks bad for the Hun. The best of it is that the Americans are doing their share of the fighting in fact probably started this counter blow. The papers are surely enthusiastic about the showing of the Americans and of the entire allied army.

Attended the dance at the officers club this evening. Had a fine time. The club used to be a girls school but is now under the auspices of the Y.M.C.A. The rooms are large and there are two good American orchestras, one upstairs and one downstairs and so continual dancing. The club is surrounded by a fine garden and soft drinks and fruit are served between dances. Lots of nice people attend the dances in fact it is a very select crowd of American Red Cross nurses, Y.M.C.A. workers, American telephone girls and some fine French people. The lady in charge passes on the eligibility of those invited and only the best people can get in. Most of the French people speak English well and it makes it very pleasant. Quite a few people have left Paris on account of the big gun "Grosse Bertha." In fact, there are many Parisians all over France. The dance is a cut in affair and the colonels and majors have to relinquish their claims on a good-looking girl if a 1st or 2nd lieutenant wants to dance with her. Was told that Ms. Nickerson from Easton, Maryland is in Tours doing Y.M.C.A. work with her mother. I have met her through her father whom I know very well in a business way. He is worth a lot of money and the daughter is a graduate of Bryn Mawr. A classmate of mine at Princeton met her at our freshman dance and later became engaged to her. He used to come to her home to see her every summer. Don't know whether they are still engaged or not as I wasn't able to locate her. Guess that she wasn't at the dance.

Tuesday, July 30th

More fellows from Italy. I find that due to a mix up in the dates some of us, myself included, have either been paid about $200.00 too little or the boys from Italy that much too much. Just my luck to be out more money. Putting through a test case and we will know before long who is right. Took a walk and went to see the movies at the "Y" this evening.

Wednesday, July 31st

Were paid today. I received 1,057 francs or $177.00 more money than I have had for a long time. Have been dead broke for six weeks. But this will not last long as I owe 200 francs for board and 250 francs for boots, etc. Money does not last long over here. Went downtown and stayed all night and had a good sleep in a good bed for a change. Had a pass until midnight but not for all night.

Thursday, August 1st

Everyone is busy watching the progress of the big battle

which looks very encouraging for the allies. We await the papers each day very eagerly. Two or three hospitals in Tours are filled with wounded Americans. They are all very enthusiastic and want to get another chance at the Boche. It is interesting to hear their tales. They all say that the Hun is a poor soldier man to man and that his morale is pretty low now. They had been told that they would be in Paris and that the war would be over this summer. And they are pretty dejected to find that it was all a lie. They didn't believe it possible for so many Americans to be over here and they were very much surprised to find the military Americans such good soldiers.

Friday, August 2nd

Rumored that some of us are going back to Foggia to fly Caproni's. Hope that it is not true or that I am not in the crowd. I prefer to go to Issoudun although they are very strict there and a person has a good chance of being kicked out of flying if he makes a little mistake. But then I would be near my French friend (Odette) and could get over to see her every weekend. Every Saturday p.m., night, and Sunday all day off at Issoudun. Very different from last winter.

Saturday, August 3rd

Went to town this evening and stayed all night at the Y.M.C.A. hotel. Tours is just like an American city and is just full of Americans. Out of 7 good hotels, four have been taken over by the Y.M.C.A., three of them being for American officers and a 4th for American telephone girls only. There are a lot of English girls and women, members of the Women's Auxiliary Corps, or WACS as we call them. It makes it very difficult to find a place to stay in Tours at all times. Tours is a flourishing business city, and it is very difficult for the French travelling trade to find lodging. But they realize that if they want America's help, they must give us a place to stay and so without a word of complaint step aside and give us the right of way. Everything here in France takes a back seat for military matters and people and everything is done to win the war. There are many high American officers here as this is headquarters. A 1st lieutenant feels rather small among majors, colonels and often generals. They are very strict about salutes here and one is kept busy saluting superior officers and returning the salutes of enlisted men. One almost needs some sort of automatic arrangement to work his arm for him.

Sunday, August 4th

Inspection at 10 a.m. Chicken dinner at 12 noon. Wrote a couple of letters and went downtown with Lancaster (12), my former roommate. He had a dinner date with a couple of French girls and so I went along. After a good dinner we took them to the theater and saw a rather good French musical comedy. After taking them home we walked to camp, something over 3 miles and got there pretty tired.

Monday, August 5th

A crowd of fellows left for Issoudun today. Lancaster (12) included. Still talk that we are to be sent to Italy again. One roommate went to the front with a squadron as a ground officer, another was sent to Brest as a ground officer in the Transportation Department and now Lancaster (12) goes to Issoudun. The best of friends sure have to part over here.

General Pershing visited this camp one day last week. Quite a good exhibition of flying was given, especially demonstrating the DeHavilland 4 with a Liberty motor. He made a short speech to the mechanics and praised their good work in the past and hoping for its continuance in the future. He said nothing to the fliers, but we do not care for we know that he does not like us at all well. He tried to have our pay reduced but failed last winter. He is an old cavalry officer and does not think that aviation is so important. However, he is waking up now and realizing how much damage can be done by enemy planes as well as our own. He had a good-sized staff with him, it is taking 3 big Hudson Super-Sixes and a Rolls Royce to carry them. It seems like home to see nice big limousines running around. There are quite a few such cars in Tours too and they sure do look good all colored drab or slate colored.

Tuesday, August 6th

Well, the unhoped for happened and all men who are at this camp and who have Farman training received orders this a.m. to return to Italy. Hate to think about going back to that hot, dirty hole of Foggia. If I should put up an awful kick, I might get out of it and be allowed to go to Issoudun. But on 2nd thought I might as well go where I am sent and not try to choose for as sure as I choose my choice will be a bad one and I will have no one to blame but myself. It has been so in the past. There are advantages on both sides. Here in France, I would have much better food, but poorer barracks; It would be near nice French people who would make life worth living; I would be among the fellows I have known longest and best in the Army; and all-around life would be more pleasant. But in Italy we will have more freedom because there are fewer of us; the type of plane I will fly there will be much safer and since it is a long war I will doubtless have a chance after to get back to France after I have had more experience and am better prepared to fly the faster type of plane. So, everything considered, I have decided to do as I am told.

Busy packing up, cleaning up, getting uniform pressed, turning in flying equipment and settling up odds and ends. I am not starting on this trip with much enthusiasm. Checked my baggage to Paris but took the train at 4:30 p.m. for Reiully to see my French friend (Odette). Most of the boys went on to Paris direct. Unfortunately, the train did not stop at Reuilly, and I had to go on to Issoudun. Got there about midnight, the train being an hour late. Trains are late all over France now. Troop trains are much more important. The Prevost Marshall lit into me for being at Issoudun without orders, but I knew him from last winter and bluffed him out. He could probably have made trouble for me.

Wednesday August 7th

Instead of getting up and going to Reuilly at 6:30 a.m., got up and had breakfast and went out to camp to see some of the boys. Got a ride out in a motorcycle side car. Saw a good many of my old friends and found Issoudun, a much-improved camp. The streets are in excellent condition and are named 5th Avenue, Broadway, 42nd Street, etc. The Red Cross and Y.M.C.A. buildings are the finest of any camp in France. Lots of planes in the air. Learned that a very good friend of mine, who had been in Italy with us, was killed yesterday. [8] He had both arms and both legs broken, and his chest crushed in. He had a wonderful constitution and lived 24 hours after the accident. He sure was a fine fellow and an excellent soldier and flyer. He got into a nosedive too close to the ground and in a cloud and couldn't get out in time. The day I left Tours a fellow I knew fairly well was killed there and another fellow badly hurt.
Took a 12:05 train to Reuilly, had dinner at a hotel where I knew the lady and her daughter very well. Then about 2:30 p.m. went round to see my friend (Odette). She was more than glad to see me as were her little sister and brother. It happened that her mother was away and would not be home until 6 o'clock. We had a great time talking things over. She said that she had been expecting me every weekend and had been very disappointed when I didn't come. I had brought 200 cigarettes from the 2.M. (Military Market) at Issoudun and gave them to her to give to her grandfather, because I knew that he was a great smoker and that it was very difficult to get cigarettes in France. Also gave her a small box of candy I had gotten for her. Had a little chewing gum with me and her kid brother sure did like it. She, her sister and myself took a walk and then met her mother at the train. I stayed for dinner until 11 p.m. and had a fine time. Big chicken dinner. An uncle, three or four aunts and her grandmother all came in to see me. It seemed like a regular reunion. Her father had left for the front just a week before after a short permission.

Thursday August 8th

Good long sleep until 9:30 a.m. Shaved and went around to see the girl (Odette) again. Her mother had gone away on an early train on business and so her sister and the two of us had 'dejeurner' or breakfast together. Then we took a long walk into the country and came back and had lunch with chicken again. A good many planes flew over town here this a.m. from the camp at Issoudun. We three took a train at 12:40 for Vierzou. I had wanted to take her and her mother to Paris to show them a good time, but her mother was unable to go today.

As I had many good friends in Reuilly, I went to say "hello!" to a couple of them before we left. At Vierzon we got a carriage and took a long trip into the country. Rode for about 2 hours or more. Pretty expensive, $3.50. Did some shopping after returning to town. Gave Odette a little medal which I had from Foggia also a U.S. pin. Gave her sister (Paulette) a little pin with a miniature rotary motor and propellor. The French are great for souvenirs.' She gave me a 4-leaf clover pin, Nenette and Rintintin and a miniature sandbag. Her little sister gave me a little white elephant. All of these things are supposed to bring good luck to a flier. Originally, they were supposed to protect the wearer from being hit by a shell in Paris. Then since the aviators dropped the bombs, these things in turn were supposed to bring good luck to allied fliers. I also bought her a pendant for her birth month (October). I didn't want her to buy me anything or give me anything but since I couldn't keep her from it, I had to give her something in return.

Her mother met us about 6 p.m. and we all visited her aunts for an hour or so and then six of us took dinner at the best hotel in town and after going back to her aunt's house for a half hour or so, I bid them goodnight and went to the hotel and hit the hay. It is very difficult to find rooms in any town in France because very many people have left Paris on account of the big gun and are staying at the hotels in all towns, small and large, round about.

Friday, August 9th

Up at 5 a.m. to catch the express for Paris at 5:50 a.m. My friends met me at the station as they were going to take a train at 6:15 a.m. My train was late as usual but theirs was too so at about 6:30 a.m. I bid them goodbye and started for Paris. Raining a little this early a.m., but it was clearing off by 8 o'clock. Could not get a seat so I had to stand up out in this aisle for a while and then I sat down on my grip. Funny, but the French are always on the go. One would hardly think it but the train so early in the a.m. was packed. Travelling at night doesn't seem to worry them at all.

While travelling thru the northern part of France a person sees as many American camps, troop trains, engines, cars, trucks, and everything as he does French. It is really remarkable the way the states have rushed men and supplies over here. One hardly knows whether he is in America or France. And the French people appreciate our efforts immensely. We passed one place which looked like a large American manufacturing town with immense warehouses, railroad yards, etc. and I am told that most of this has been done in the last 3 months. The German offensive surely did speed things up. Passed through Orleans on our way to Paris. Reached the Quai d'Orsay at Paris about 10 a.m. It took me until about 11 a.m. to get my baggage located and transferred by taxi clear across the city to the Gare de Lyon. Was to meet a fellow at the Café de la Paix at 10:30 a.m., but he was not there. Had dinner at the Hotel Richmond which is run by the Y.M.C.A. Saw many old friends there among them the 2nd lieutenant who had brought us down to Italy. Now it was his turn to salute me as I was a 1st lieutenant instead of a cadet. Also saw my old instructor at Ft. Myer. He was a 1st lieutenant last August and is now a major. That's the way they are jumping in the regular army but not in the Reserves. This war has made colonels and brigadier generals out of young fellows who in peace times would be 1st or 2nd lieutenants.

After dinner I drove out to headquarters to try to get some money which I had coming to me for mileage (some $45.00). Unfortunately, the check had been mailed to me 3 days before. I needed money pretty badly so went to the American University Union where I knew a classmate of mine was a secretary. There I met many college and Ground School friends and also found him. He gave me the dope on several of the boys and he keeps a "Dope" book for "1916" and in it I read much real news about classmates. Found one classmate who had come back from the front. He had been in the infantry but was going to train as an aerial observer. He had many interesting tales to tell. As to the money, I didn't have a blank check, didn't have any money in the bank or a thing but he wrote out a check with a typewriter and I signed it, and he endorsed it. The check was for $50.00, and I wired Papa to take care of it when I reached home since it was on the 1st National of Saltsburg. Will send him the money when I get paid again.

After a good chat with the boys, the fellow from the front and myself did a bit of shopping and then drove around town to see the sights. Saw the Place de Concorde, Arc de Triumphe, Champs Elysée's, Grand Palais, Petit Palais, Les Invalides, Notre-Dame, the Eiffel Tower, and many other places. Of course, we did not have time to go in any of these places. Came back and had dinner with cake and ice cream. Impossible to get ice cream except where Americans manage things. Saw several more friends at dinner, a boy named Robinson from Newark, N.J. He was in my battery at Ft. Myer. Caught the train at 8:05 p.m. for Marseilles and Nice. Had not thought to engage a seat so it looked as if I would have to stand up as they were all reserved. I had a 24-hour ride too. By tipping the conductor, however, I got a seat before long. The price for a sleeper for one night was about $17.00. Too rich for my blood.

Saturday, August 10th

After a night of drowsing and trying to sleep sitting up; I woke up feeling pretty bum this a.m. Had breakfast in the dining car and felt quite a bit better. Fairly nice country along here. This is about the fastest and best train between Paris and Marseilles. We are about 1 hour late. Arrived at Marseilles about noon. Stopped there for a short time. Marseilles is the 3rd city of France in size but is like most seaport towns rather dirty. After leaving Marseilles I had lunch on the train. Two fellows going to Foggia got on at Marseilles and I found out that another got on at Paris. There are probably 20 Americans on the train altogether, mostly officers. A couple of them are lucky enough to be going back to the states after a leave at Nice. Met one fellow who was wounded and gassed at the front. He is in bad condition and very nervous. Has been in a hospital for some time. There is a very nice French civilian in my compartment. He is on 3 months leave as he has been badly wounded at the front twice. He is a flyer and did exhibition flying in the states in 1910. He has been all over the world and is very interesting to talk with. He speaks English very well. He is going to see his wife in Nice. His home is in Paris, but she is down in Nice on account of the bombardment of Paris. The big gun was playing on Paris the day I was there, but no shells hit near where I was. Saw the results of their work in several places.

This is the most wonderful country I have ever seen. We are right along the Mediterranean and there are countless big hotels, resorts, and villas. Swimming places all along. Surely is picturesque. Arrived in Nice at 6 p.m., went to the hotel, took a bath and a shave, and had dinner. It seems that we are at a very expensive hotel as dinner was some $4.00 apiece. After dinner we took a stroll along the Riviera, which is just like the Atlantic City boardwalk and enjoyed the sea breezes. Very warm down here. No lights along the Riviera for fear of air raids and submarines. Took in sort of a musical revue at one of the big hotels and then hit the hay about midnight.

Sunday, August 11th

Slept until late the a.m. When I did wake up, I found that the mosquitoes had about eaten me up. My one eye was swelled clear shut. This happened to me a couple of times in the states too. I sure did look a sight until about 1 or 2 p.m. and then it was about all gone. Took a stroll along the beach and drove up to the station to see about my baggage before lunch. Did not eat any breakfast at all and took lunch at a hotel where the Y.M.C.A. prices prevailed, and they suited my pocketbook better. After lunch spent awhile in the British Y.M.C.A. and then went bathing. It is too hot to bathe around noon time. Stayed in a bathing suit until 6:30 p.m. Then had dinner, took a stroll along a walk, and then went to the casino which is a very large pavilion built over the ocean. Good movies and a good concert. We requested and the orchestra played a couple of American pieces. Lots of Americans here in Nice. Some of them have lived here for years. Met a Mrs. Wheatley from Washington D.C. who has lived in Nice for 16 years. She sure treated me fine, gave me her card and told me to be sure and look her up if I ever came back to Nice. She said that Nice was more interesting in the winter since the better people came there then. She said that it was too hot at this time. In the winter there is an officer's club where dances, etc. are held. Mrs. Hunter, who is a big society lady, has opened her residence for this purpose but just at present is out of town for a few weeks. Mrs. Wheatley was sorry that I was leaving so soon and told me that she would see that I had a good time and meet some nice people if I came back. Met several old college friends and was introduced to Eddie Hart probably the greatest football player that ever went to Princeton. He was captain of the team for 2 years, one year being 1911 when Princeton won the championship. He played that year with a broken neck regardless of the doctors' orders. He has an awful neck and chest and wore a plaster of Paris cast all that season. He is conceded to be the strongest man in the world, having recently defeated a big Pole in Paris who had beaten all comers for years.

Nice is surely one fine place, better than Asbury Park or Atlantic City. I imagine that it is like Palm Beach. The society of France, England and Italy come there in peace times. Wonderful big hotels, some of which are closed now until winter. The casino is a great gambling hall as is the noted Casino at Monte Carlo.

Monday, August 12th

Up at 6:30 a.m., had breakfast and caught the train at 8:15 a.m. for Genoa. Beautiful scenery all along the coast. Never seen anything more picturesque than the villas and hotels along the mountainous coast. Passed thru Monaco and Monte Carlo, both which are beautiful. Had expected to visit Monte Carlo yesterday but didn't get time. At Menton, just before we came to the border, the train stopped for an hour and a half, and we all filed through several offices to have our passports examined. The hand luggage of civilians was searched here. Gee! But it was hot and there was an awful crush. Then again, we stopped at Ventimiglia just on the other side of the border and the baggage of civilians was all torn open and thoroughly examined. Stopped here for 2 hours and got lunch. We knew we were in Italy because we had spaghetti for lunch. Thank goodness we were able to check our baggage clear through to Foggia from here. Baggage is so much trouble over here and gets lost so easily. It costs about as much to carry a trunk with you as it does for your ticket. Baggage does not go free as in America. Left here about 3 p.m. and arrived in Genoa at 11 a.m. Left there at 12 for Rome. The coast clear down to Genoa is beautiful.

Tuesday, August 13th

We did our best to get a sleeper to Rome but couldn't. Impossible even to get a seat and I wasn't feeling all too well. Stomach out of whack and I spent too much time running to the toilet. Felt sort of weak. Sat on my valise in the aisle for a while then lay right down on the floor on my overcoat. People walked right over me, and one woman stepped right in my face. Managed to find a seat about 4 a.m. and slept sitting up until about 8 a.m. Sure was tired out. Got some boiled eggs and bread at a station and ate them for breakfast. Dozed all morning until we reached Rome at 11 a.m. Some famous American socialista, Sprague Russell and a couple of others got off the same train and were given quite a reception. Tried to get a berth to Foggia but all gone as usual. Was heading for a hotel when two fellows who were going to Foggia saw me and struck me for some money. Said that their pockets had been picked. Gave them $18.00 or $20.00 in turn was given the use of their rooms at the Royal Hotel. Shaved and got cleaned up and had dinner with them. Then went to bed as I was feeling poor and slept to 5 o'clock, got up and had dinner with the crowd and pulled out for Foggia at 7:30 p.m.

Wednesday, August 14th

After another night sitting up sleeping, we arrived in Foggia at 5:30 a.m. I was half sick and awfully tired. Got cab out to camp and had breakfast. Baggage not here yet. Spent most of the day sleeping. Very few boys here. Not more than 25 of most of them ready to leave in a day or two. We were sent down here on account of the shortage of men here, so the order read. Got a little settled today and got blankets, sheets, flying clothes, etc. issued to us. To bed at dark this evening.

Thursday, August 15th

Up at 7 a.m. and had breakfast. There is a rule that everybody has to keep out of the barracks from 7:30 to 10 a.m. for fresh air purposes. Doctors orders. Most of us read or write outside. I wrote 3-4 letters today. Got 3 from the French girl (Odette). Quick work, eh what? The commandant was pretty sore because we took so long coming down and called us down quite a bit, but nothing more will be said, I think. The quarters are excellent with good iron beds, mattresses, sheets, pillows and pillowcases, mosquito bars, etc. Flies are awful. Eats are fair for Foggia but nothing like France.

Friday, August 16th

Read most of the day. Too lazy to take any exercise. Twenty men put on flying list, but my name is away down the list alphabetically. Several machines were busted up lately so there are only two left for 2 lines. Better than we thought, however, for we had heard that there were no planes at all and that there wouldn't be until September 1st. To bed early again.

Saturday, August 17th

Read a lot again today. Ice cream at the Y this p.m. @ 1 lira or about $.15 a dish. Sure tasted good. Have not been feeling well at all and the doctor gave me a couple of doses of castor oil. After spending a pretty miserable day yesterday am feeling better today. Had a light case of dysentery! Went downtown to do some shopping this evening. Could find only a couple of the articles I wanted and had to pay these robbers two or three prices for them. Surely am disgusted with this hole which smells worse than ever and with these people. Came back and went to bed early.

Sunday, August 18th

Stomach not right yet and am feeling poor again today. Think the bad water started me and then it is mighty hot down here. If I don't feel better soon, I will go to the hospital for treatment as the "doc" says such trouble is dangerous in a hot climate like this.

Monday, August 19th

Feeling better today. Read a lot, almost all day long. Read Galsworthy's' "Beyond" which is mighty good.

Received check for milage up to France ($44.04). Needed it badly.

Tuesday, August 20th

Read and slept all day. Awfully lazy life, in fact a person just lies around and nearly rots. Don't know how I will ever be able to work after the war if I get back to the states. Along that line we have a song which runs something like this:

"Take me over the seas, where the wild violets can't get at me, the "jay-cats" they whistle, The Sopwiths they roar, I don't want to ride in Farman's no more."
Rather poor, eh what? Don't remember the word very well.

I want to go home,
I want to go home,
The "Jay-cats" they whistle,
The Sopwiths they roar,
I don't want to ride the Farman's no more,
Take me over the sea,
Where the wild violets can't get to me.
Oh! My. I'm too young to die.
I want to go home

There are 2 other verses, but I don't remember the words. Of course, that is all a joke.

Wednesday, August 21st

Wrote several letters and read a lot more today. Read Rupert Hughes "What Will People Say?" Very good book. We learned this a.m. that 3 Italians who were flying a Caproni over from Naples to this camp were killed last night when forced to land on a mountain top. A crowd of fellows were sent to Turin to fly "600" Capronis come back again today. Got only as far as Rome. As usual the Wops did not have the school ready for them. So instead of getting up to the civilized part of Italy such as Milan or Turin it looks as if we would stay in this god forsaken place until we are all ready for the front.

Have been here only a week and have received six letters from Odette and one from her kid sister (Paulette) already. Going some, eh what? According to French custom each letter contains some pressed flowers, different colors having differ meanings, I have received all colors I believe. Her little sister tried to write in English and although I understood it OK, it was about the funniest letter I ever read.

Thursday, August 22nd

More reading and letter writing today. Will probably be flying soon. Am expecting a package of eats soon which Odette has sent. The eats are getting awfully old now. No variety at all because it is hard to buy the stuff in Foggia and there is no American commissary in Italy as yet. American troops and fliers are on the Italian front, and I think that there will be an American 2.M. (Military Market) in Italy soon. We are paying an exorbitant rate for board too, 10 liras a day. In normal times a lira and a franc are equal about $.19. A franc is now about $.17.5 whereas a lira was as low as $.11 last winter. We paid 5 francs a day in France or about $.85 a day, while down here the board is much poorer and at the present rate of exchange we are paying about $1.50 per day. The commandant and staff officers have better mess and better service and pay only 7 liras. It isn't right but it is another case of being rooked in a different way. What is probably happening is that some of these Wops are getting rebates downtown from the merchants. Our mess officer is forced to pay a high price for things and then certain fellows on the inside get a rake-off from the merchants. And the mess is poor too. Eggs and rice for breakfast, possibly meat and potatoes, lemonade and fruit for lunch and soup and spaghetti or eggs and potatoes again for dinner. No variety at all and soup and that stuff is too greasy and hot for this kind of weather.

Very foolish to send us up to France and bring us back again with about $55.00 mileage each way. Then too we only got from 3 to 6 hours flying up there in two months. A waste of time and money that's all. But it is another case of the government changing its mind for this school was to be closed up for Americans. Then the policy was altered. Hence, we are here again.

Friday, August 23rd

Instead of reading so much I wrote five letters today. They were selling ice cream at the "Y" this p.m. and it sure did taste good in this hot weather. We just got word thru letters today that three fellows who had been down here with us at West camp last fall and winter had been killed at Issoudun. One was a boy named Sutton (14) from Pittsburgh and an excellent flier. His father was a big steel man and worth all kind of money. Another was a boy named Hamilton (15) from Columbus Ohio, also a very good flier. A third named Schreiber (16), another very good flier. It seems that the best fliers get killed off first. It may be because they take more chances. Eight fellows were killed in 6 days at Issoudun just after we left France. Picking them off pretty fast for only training. They had a funeral for four in one day up there. At the front is where the boys really get knocked off. In a squadron of 17 men at the front they average 8 replacements a week, which means that the average man lasts two weeks at the front. Of course, some fear may by chance last lots longer. And General Pershing wanted to reduce our pay because he claimed that aviation is no more dangerous than any other branch of the service. While on this subject I forgot to mention the death of another boy named Phyllis [9]from Illinois. He was killed at Tours while I was still on the flying list there. Saw his machine come down until it was lost from sight behind the trees. It looked as if he would make a safe enough landing but when they found him his neck was broken as were his jaws. The doctor said that he had a good place to land and should not have been hurt at all. But you never can tell and the more I think of it the luckier I think that I was not to have gotten hurt when I fell. The day before we left Tours a boy named Bradford (13) who I knew slightly was killed. His motor went bad while he was doing a renversement pretty close to the ground.

Saturday, August 24th

Wrote six letters today and did a little reading. Put in an application for flying pay which I have not as yet received. Should have been getting it long ago and would have been if I had stayed in the states. So instead of drawing $220.00 per month as I should be, I am only getting $177.00. But will be able to collect the extra back for a couple of months I believe. We are all kicking about the mess both the quality and the price of it. Don't know what can be done. Found out yesterday that I had the French itch. Probably got it from the beds up there. It comes from the trenches. Am doctoring it and rubbing myself every night with mercury and sulfur. It bothered me so much that I have only gotten about 3 hours of sleep a night for three nights now.

Sunday, August 25th

Wrote five letters today and am beginning to get caught up with my correspondence. George H. Prenner of York, PA, whom I knew very well, was killed this a.m. in a Caproni. He is the first man to be killed in a Caproni here at this camp and some 150 men have been trained here. I left N.Y. with him, bunked right close to him at Issoudun for 3 months, was with him at West Camp for 4 months, trained at Tours with him and came down here two weeks ago with him. So, you see that I knew him very well. Worked with him on the same cooking force at Issoudun. In fact, he was one of my best friends here now. He got into a sideslip, then a vrille and then the plane turned over and came down on him upside down with motors full on. The gas tank cut his head in two. The gas tank broke and saturated him with gasoline and his body was burned black. Fortunately, he was undoubtedly dead before he burned up. The plane burned to ashes. It is really too bad but this game is dangerous and so we must expect things like this. His fiancée's heart will be broken. He was telling me just two days ago about her turning another fellow down lately, a fellow who had money and could buy her anything she wanted. But she preferred to wait for him.

Monday, August 26th

Funeral at 8:00 a.m. and we all marched to Foggia and then to the cemetery. Very hot and dusty. After a number of a fellows good friends have been killed and wounded, he begins to take this war personally and feels like avenging the deaths of his friends. The Kaiser can be directly blamed for all of this.

The funeral was nicely conducted. They do not use a hearse but a wagon, something like a big dray wagon with three horses. An Italian bodyguard precedes the wagon then the pall bearers walk alongside the wagon, then comes the American bodyguard and last a body of Italian soldiers. The casket is covered with an American flag. Two Caproni planes circled over the procession all the way to the cemetery; also, another smaller plane, an Ansaldo S.V.A. biplane. Up at Issoudun planes usually circle over the procession and drop wreaths on the grave. A boy got some pictures of the funeral, and I expect to get some from him. The commandant read the service at the grave followed by the blowing of "taps" over the grave. After the funeral I stayed in town and did a little shopping.

Tuesday, August 27th

Kept busy writing letters and reading again today. Last night about midnight the alarm was sounded, and it was reported that we were going to have an air raid. We all jumped into our clothes in a jiffy and were out of the barracks. Orders are always given to get away from the buildings and to scatter in case of a raid because they always drop their bombs on buildings. It was a bright moonlight night and fine for a raid. The planes crossed the coast but did not reach here. We had heard today that they had raided a town 15 or 20 miles away. All we saw were a lot of flares or rockets sent up as warnings all around Foggia and vicinity. One searchlight at Foggia and one here at camp swept the sky for a half an hour. Antiaircraft guns were tested, and a plane was sent up from camp here and flew around for about an hour. We had several such scares last spring, but nothing ever came of them. The Germans and Austrians have us exactly located, however.

Wednesday, August 28th

Went down to a show at the Sala Italia last night. It was much better than usual and one of the singers was plainly above the average of this circuit. She was Spanish I believe. It rained pretty hard during the show. We sure needed it for it has been terribly hot and dusty. We had a regular windstorm yesterday p.m. and everything including ourselves was just covered with dust. We had a hard time finding the carriage last night at 10:30. It used to be easy to find one as late as 12 o'clock but guess most of these robbers have gotten rich off the Americans. One of the bankers downtown was telling a friend of mine that the Americans had put a wonderful amount of money in circulation and that the merchants were very sorry to hear that this camp was to be given up by the Americans and were overjoyed when it was decided not to abandon it. One boot shop downtown made so much money that the proprietor has closed up shop and retired. That's the way these robbers appreciate the Americans who have come 3 or 4 thousand miles to fight their battles. It is so different from France!

Wrote several letters today. Expect to get on the flying list tomorrow or the next day. The propellor broke with a fellow up in the air this a.m. and a piece went into the gas tank. The fellow was saturated with gasoline but kept his head and made a good landing. Lucky that the plane didn't take fire, or we would have been going to another funeral.

Thursday, August 29th

Wrote several letters again today. Took a long walk this evening. One of the boys got a letter from Issoudun today saying that another boy, Arthur Preyer (17), was killed. He went out for an hours flight and was found shortly after in a dying condition. He is from Holland and his people live at the Hague. He came to Princeton in the fall of 1916 when he couldn't speak any English at all, made good as a soccer player and was elected captain of the team his sophomore year. He also made one of the 3 best clubs at Princeton, all of which speaks very well for him since he came there unable to speak English at all. I knew him very well and he was a dandy fellow. He was in my battery at Fort Myer and at Princeton Ground School; he was here at Foggia last spring and at Tours last month with me. We also heard that several others had met with accidents at Issoudun lately. Bill Gould (18) from Hastings-on-Hudson, N.Y. had most of his teeth knocked out and his jaws badly hurt. I knew him in training camp, Ground school and was with him until a month ago. Charlie Schminke from Massachusetts had his leg broken; knew him well too. Harry Moses (19) had his leg hurt. He is from Texas, and I have been with him for 10 months. Donat Pepin (20) from Michigan had his hand badly burnt; have known him for 10 months too. They sure are treating the boys pretty rough.

Friday, August 30th

No flying today. Too much wind. It is exceptionally hard to handle a Caproni in a strong wind because it has 3 enormous rudders, and it takes lots of strength in the legs to bring them back to neutral once they get out. Read a lot today.

Saturday, August 31st

Still too much wind for flying. Too bad because there are some 25 of us here who haven't flown this month, and this is the last day. A fellow has to get 3 or 4 flights a month to draw flying pay which is $41.50 for a 1st lieutenant. So, you see it makes quite a difference although we may get it anyhow. It is not our fault at all because we are ready and willing to fly, and we can't help the fact that there are only enough planes for the first half of the alphabet. My name has kept me out of several good things in the army where it is impossible to consider the individual. We are all tired of this monkey business and most of us don't care much what happens. We came over here all filled with pep and eager to get to the front as soon as possible but we fooled around so long that we don't care no more. It is not my fault that I have gotten only 22 ½ hours flying in 10 whole months over here. I have flown in good shape and am right in with the crowd I left the states with. I have gone just as fast as they gave me a chance to. Too bad our air force has not come nearly up to expectations. I would have gotten much flying in a week in the states as I have over here in 10 months. And to think I turned down the chance to train at Mineola, Long Island or Essington, N.J.

Sunday, September 1st

No flying at all on Sunday anymore. Loafed all day as usual. Further news of a boy named Donald Yund (21) from Ohio who had a crash at Issoudun and is not expected to live. We all eagerly watch the papers for the progress of the battle up in France. The allies are surely driving them back. They have gained in 6 weeks two thirds of what it took the Germans 4 months to capture. The German army seems to be demoralized. The English papers published in Paris don't reach us until 4 or 5 days late, but we read the Italian papers and then too the official communiques come in daily giving the results of the previous day's fighting. They are all translated and the large wall maps in the Y.M.C.A. changed accordingly, i.e. I mean the strings indicating the different lines are changed daily.

Monday September 2nd

Labor Day, but no holiday for the army. Everyday has been a holiday for us lately. Lists posted and I begin flying tomorrow; surely am glad for I am sick and tired lying around doing nothing. We also are to have some ground school classes beginning tomorrow. Two hours a week on motors and two more on rigging of the plane. Good stuff and something to occupy one's mind. Classes are 2:30 – 3:30 p.m. daily. I am Officer of the Day today. Reported to the office and received instructions at 11 a.m. from the Adjutant. Inspected the mess at 5 p.m. Have to inspect quarters and see that everyone is in bed at 10 p.m. and all lights out. Then I have to get up at 5 a.m. to see that fliers are up at 5:30 a.m. and non-fliers by 7 a.m. Then I inspect quarters at 7:30 a.m. to see that everyone is outside of barracks and then again at 9:30 a.m. to see that they are still outside. From 7:30 – 10 a.m. everyone is supposed to be outside to get fresh air. In case of an air raid, I am supposed to see that everyone gets out of the barracks promptly. At 11 a.m. tomorrow I will be through and another O.D. will come on duty.

Tuesday, September 3rd

Was awake early this a.m. as I had to get the other boys up. I told the cook last night to wake me at 5 o'clock, which he did but it wasn't necessary for I was afraid that he would forget and so I was awake about 4:30 a.m. It was dark up until 6 o'clock so I did not awaken the rest until that time. At inspection last night I found one man absent, but he was downtown on business. All was O.K. at 7:30 and the 10:30 inspection this morning. Reported to the office and was relieved from duty as O.D. at 11 a.m. Strange to say I didn't get balled out; usually a fellow gets that on general principle whether he deserves it or not. At 11:30 a.m. there was a meeting of all officers of the post in the Y.M.C.A. A general order was read to us about the German spy system and how thorough it is. We were cautioned to keep our mouths shut and if anyone is caught talking and giving out information in public or to anyone, he will be court martialed. This is right because we are all prone to talk and brag too much.

We had our 1st class this p.m. in rigging. I learned quite a bit about the gasoline, air, and water systems, also about the wiring of the whole plane. The principal thing I learned was just how to shut off the gasoline in case a motor catches on fire in the air. Being burned to death is about as mean a way to die as I know and there have been quite a number of instances with these Capronis here, where the pilot or pilots got down just in time to save their own lives but not in time to save the planes. We did not get started to fly today because it was very windy, but we hope to tomorrow.

Wednesday September 4th

The new dual-control lines started this a.m. so we were up and out at 6 o'clock. I had a good joy ride although it lasted only 6 minutes. There are 10 men on our line, and we have an Italian sergeant for an instructor. He seems good and not so excitable as most Wops. Still good news from France. The Allies are continually pushing the Germans back and it looks now as if they couldn't stop until they reach the old Hindenburg line and possibly not then.

Thursday September 5th

I got another ride today. These planes are O.K. but are terribly large and with three motors to watch a person almost has to be an expert mechanic to get away with it. The Caproni is very easy to fly as long as the motors all work well but when one goes bad it is very hard to control sometimes on account of its great weight. If the rudders get away or the plane commences to sideslip due to too steep a bank or a motor going bad; it is much harder to control because of its weight. Then too since its wingspread is so large, it is very difficult at first to know when you are flying exactly level. This doesn't matter much in the air but in making a landing if one wing is low it may scrape the ground and break. So, it takes a very delicate sense of balance to handle one of these planes.

Friday September 6th

Good flying weather again today and I had two lessons, one in the a.m. and one in the p.m. I made or tried to make 4 landings. I always redress too soon and make the landing "up in the air" so to speak. These planes land very fast, and the tendency is to pull up too soon because you have the idea that you are going to drive right into the ground. It is an altogether different landing from what I have been used to up in France so it will be a little while before I get onto it. Everyone has the same trouble more or less. The "Y" showed some movies of the fighting up in France this evening, but they were only fairly good.

Saturday September 7th

Flying this a.m. but I did not get up because the instructor spent a lot of time with the 1st two men and sent them solo. They both did O.K. Then while flying with the 3rd man one of the motors caught on fire and they had to land. So, the flying ended for the morning and this evening it was too windy. Our instructor wants to finish us all up and go on leave, so he sends us solo when we barely know how to land the bus and know very little about flying it. The two boys this a.m. soloed after 45 – 50 minutes dual-control work while the men who have the American instructors get from 2 – 3 hours of much better instruction before soloing. We get 5 lessons, and they get from 10 – 15 so we are at quite a disadvantage and haven't nearly so much confidence until we learn things for ourselves. The boy who was killed the other day[10] had been instructed by our instructor and so didn't know enough about flying the bus.

Sunday September 8th

Sunday and no flying today. Read, wrote letters and slept for most of the day. Had a good game of tennis this evening but I haven't played for so long that I am rather stale. A good many of the boys went downtown tonight. I noticed by the paper today that the Manpower Bill has been passed calling all men from the ages of 18 – 45. Sorry to know that it takes in both Art and Hal, also Ralph. Wish that I could be at home to give the boys some advice. If I had been able to get some good advice I would not be where I am or doing what I am and would have done better to stay in the Artillery I believe. We fellows over here are glad that the Government is getting a lot of the slackers back home. It doesn't go good to hear that ordinary laborers are getting \$8 - \$10 a day and that many mill workers, shipbuilders etc. are getting \$10 - \$20 a day and undergo no danger while the poor doughboy gets \$1 a day and is in constant peril of his life. But "War is H---!" and this is just another of its bad features.

Monday September 9th

"Troppo vento" (too much wind) and no flying today. Read and played cards quite a bit. Don't know hardly what to do with myself. This life gets on a person's nerves. There is nothing to do and no nice people in Foggia and because of training it is impossible to get a leave. Ice Cream at the "Y" this p.m. They have it there about 3 times a week. It costs a lira or 18 cents a dish; rather dear but the least it can be made for down here. We all raised an awful kick about the price of board a few days ago and I think the price has been reduced from 10 – 8 lira a day which helps some. And then too the grub seems better than before. It shows what can be done when someone takes a little interest.

Tuesday September 10th

Too bumpy for flying this a.m. and it really was this evening too, but we flew anyhow. I got up and had two landings but did not learn much for it was so rough that the instructor couldn't give me much control. I did several things wrong, and he got a little sore at me. All Wops are excitable, so I didn't mind it at all. The Haas boy who wrote to the Greensburg paper has just gotten back from France where he went to see his brother who is in a hospital in Limoges. His brother is a Captain in the Infantry and knows Bob Woodend. He himself has been badly gassed but is getting better. He will not be sent to the front again but will be kept in the S.O.S. He said that Bob W--- had been slightly wounded but was well again. I follow the casualties lists very closely and the last few days I have seen the names of many fellows from near home, some from Blairsville, Vandergrift, Salina, Iselin, Indiana, Greensburg, Derry, Latrobe, Homer City, Uniontown etc. Noticed the death of Harry Empfield and some Levine from Blairsville, a Clawson from Indiana and a Rupert from Salina.

Wednesday September 11th

Windy and bumpy and so no flying today. This life is surely getting monotonous. Read a very good book today entitled "The European War – 2nd Phase" or "Battle of the Marne" (1914). It was wonderfully interesting, although Joffre was commander-in-chief, it was General Foch who really saved the day. Even as early as 1914 this author, Helaire Beloc, one of the two greatest military critics, considered Foch the greatest allied general. It is queer that the allies didn't realize this several years ago and give him supreme command. Since he has had full power, it has been a different story. Just along this line, it seems as if the Germans have decided to make a stand on the old Hindenburg line for, they are counterattacking, and the Allies are going slower. In seven weeks, the Allies have retaken all the territory the Germans had taken in four months this summer. For the past month there has been a lot of talk of an American offensive in the Toul sector. I think that it will come off soon. Of course, the Americans have been doing their full share along with the French and British with whom they are brigaded but the independent American Army of about 800,000 men is in the Toul sector. Of course, we are all anxious to see them take grips with the Hun. The principal trouble with the Americans seems to be that they go too fast, i.e., this is what the British and French say. The French all just adore the Americans, and a British Officer told me that he would like to see the American army placed between the French and the British so that they could both get some inspiration from it. Coming from a Britisher this statement means something for he doesn't grant a foreigner anything he doesn't have to. The Americans get along much better with the French than the English do.

Thursday September 12th

Still no flying on account of the wind. It is a bit early for the equinoctial storms and winds, but this is surely something unusual. Last Spring it often blew for 2 or 3 days at a time but here we have had a bad week of this without a drop of rain. News came from Milan today that David Reynolds (22) was killed there in a 600 H.P. Caproni along with an Italian pilot. The control motor fell out and cut off the tail, so they had no control of the plane at all. I knew Reynolds (22) very well; his home is in Montclair N.J., and he was in my company and my battery at Fort Myer. He went to Princton Ground School and was here at Foggia last winter.

Friday September 13th

Friday the 13th and still she blows and no flying. News reached here by telegraph that the American offensive has started on the Toul sector. Hope Friday the 13th may prove lucky for the boys. They started off fine by taking 5 miles and over 5,000 prisoners the first day. A fellow just came down from Tours today and said the offensive was expected up in France and that lots of American fliers, many of them my friends, were being rushed up to the front at once to take part in the drive. Many of them are flying De Havilland planes with Liberty motors. Our West Camp boys, i.e., the ones who didn't get killed or hurt, are doing very well up in France and most of them are going chasse (hunting). A friend of mine who went to the front from Issoudun last March has eight Huns to his credit and a D.S.C. (Distinguished Service Cross) He is about 20 years old and some flier. News also came today 13,500,000 had registered yesterday in the States and that an army of 4,000,000 would be maintained on the Western Front. With 23,500,000 men registered for the draft it looks bad for Germany.

Found out today that our board is still costing us 10 liras or at the present rate of exchange $1.40 a day. The reason is that "26" enlisted men eat with us and the Government. only allows them 5 liras a day. There are about fifty of us officers, so you see we pay or contribute 2 ½ lira a day each to furnish grub for the enlisted men. I dare say that this is the only post where officers pay for enlisted men's mess. When we were cadets at Ground School the Government allowed us only 60 cents per day and to obtain $1 a day mess we paid 40 cents out of our own pockets. Also, at West Camp last

Winter when the mess was so rotten, we had to pay out of our own pockets for eggs, etc. It isn't right when 8 or 10 staff officers have their own mess and pay only 7 lira a day and they are the ones that force us to pay 10 liras a day and so contribute to the enlisted men's mess. Of course, we don't begrudge them what they eat but we would rather have the Government. foot the bill if they are to eat officers mess. We can't do anything for the doctor has forbidden us to eat outside of the camp and so they have us for we can't starve.

Took a walk downtown last night for exercise and expect to again tonight. I paid 95 cents (5 liras) for a bottle of ink last night. Could get it for 10 cents, possibly 5 cents in the States. Pretty dear, eh what?

Saturday September 14th

Still very windy and so no flying. Having been doing odd and ends which I had put off all along during this period of idleness. More good news from France. The Americans have advanced some twenty miles (150 square miles), have taken 200 guns and 15,000 prisoners. This was all done in 27 hours and is said to be a record for speed over here. It was to be expected that the Americans should do their job in a hurry for in the U.S. we move at least two or three times as fast as they do over here, All the papers, French, English, and Italian speak in great praise of the U.S. troops for this work.

Sunday, September 15th

It looks as if we would never get to flying again for it is windier today than ever. Took a walk downtown this evening and went to the movies which were fairly good. Saw a few very nice people, i.e., nice for Foggia.

Monday, September 16th

The wind had died down this a.m., but when we have flying weather something else is wrong; it seems for only one plane out of eleven would fly this a.m. It is the old Wop system of slowness and too the fact that the planes are all worn out. It is very seldom that one of these motors will go at top speed for any length of time at all without back firing and catching on fire in the carburetor or something breaking. The Americans in charge of the school said this a.m. that he was going to do his best to close up the school within the next months. This has been tried before but our government seems bent on keeping it going for propaganda purposes. It is really a crime to waste so much time and to make us fly such rickety, old machines. We were also told that the oil was practically done and that there was none in sight. So quite a few of the boys asked the Captain for leave but he refused all but one of them. I was very sorry not to get a ride this a.m. for I would have gotten it with a very good American instructor because my Wop instructor was away for the day. I am not learning much from him anyhow. He is set on going on leave very soon and is trying to turn us solo when we don't know hardly anything about the ship. It is not fair to us to be getting about 1/3 of the instruction the other fliers get. Oil, a little came, and we flew this evening. I had one ride, and the motor went bad, so it didn't count as a lesson. It is the same old hard luck. It looks as though we are interned here for the duration of the war.

Tuesday, September 17th

Flying today and I did awfully rotten. As I said before, my Wop instructor wants to go on leave and is so bound to solo us or to turn in a report that we can't fly a Caproni. He gave me 9 landings, but I didn't do well enough to solo, and he is raving mad. He swore at me something fierce and called me all of the names he could think of. The last landing we managed to break a couple of wires on the plane. He got me more and more nervous as we went along. I could have done better all alone. I feel sure for he would wave his hands in the air and curse just as I was making a landing and would rattle me. I expected to be kicked off altogether, but another fellow told me that he would give me one more lesson and if I did not do OK, I would be kicked off. I knew that I wouldn't get along with him, so I decided not to go up with him again and I went to see the American officer in charge of training, and he told me to fly with the American instructor. He said that they were wise to the Wop and realized that he wasn't giving us a square deal. I thought for a while that my flying career might be ruined by this boob, but I think that all will be OK now.

Wednesday, September 18th

Flying this a.m. but I was sick and so didn't go out. The Wop was looking for me, but I told him that I was sick. I had a long talk with the American with whom I will fly, and he treated me fine and he told me not to fly

AERO CLUB D'ITALIA

Sotto l'alto patronato di S. M. il Re

(F. A. I.)

BREVETTO SUPERIORE

DI

Pilota Aviatore

Riconosciuto dall'Autorità Militare

G. TOSSO ROMA

2nd Brevet Certification

Stewart's Italian Aviator Badge

Regio Esercito Italiano

COMANDO SCUOLE AVIATORI

Il Tenente

Robinson Samuel S

del Air Service U-S-A

è autorizzato a fregiarsi del distintivo istituito col R. Decreto 21 maggio 1916, N. 641.

Il Il Tenente Colonnello Comandante delle Scuole Aviatori

COMANDO SCUOLE AVIATORI

E. Chiri [signature]

Above: Stewart's Italian Aviator Wings.

until I felt OK. I have the Spanish influenza, in fact. I had it all day yesterday and that probably helps account for my poor showing. The hospital is full of patients with the "flu." One of the doctors and a couple of the instructors have it. The camp has been under quarantine since Sunday because Foggia is full of it. I have a headache, sore throat, and ache quite a bit but have not gone to the hospital yet. Took some aspirin and had my throat sprayed this a.m. The Wop turned another fellow solo this a.m. and he nearly broke the machine and another of his pupils broke one up very badly thus evening. It is just a case of sending a man solo before he is ready. On the other hand, a fellow whom the Wop said would never be able to handle a Caproni and so turned off his line after 4 lessons, took 2 lessons with an American and laid down two perfect landings flying solo. It just goes to show that the Wop has no judgment at all and so they will not take his word. The American commandant and the Wop commandant had a big confab yesterday and the Italians were given to understand where they belonged, and that this instructor was not doing the right thing.

Thursday, September 19th

Still sick today and so didn't fly. Feel about the same as I did yesterday. More fellows are getting sick every day. The adjutant got it today. I asked for a day's leave to go down to Bari to take a swim for tomorrow is a national holiday in Italy. The Captain said no. The baseball team left here at midnight tonight for Rome where they play Saturday. They will be back Monday a.m. The track team left last night and will compete in Rome on Friday the 20th.

Previous Page: Stewart's Italian Aviator Certificate (Note: The date referenced on the certificate is not the date of the award, but rather it is the date that the award was established.)

Friday, September 20th

No flying today as it is a holiday. I believe that it is the date in the year 1860 when the Italian people under Garibaldi took Rome from the Pope. The Italian officers gave a little tea or reception this evening at 5 p.m. for the American officers. It was a pretty lively affair, I guess from what I hear. I was feeling pretty poor and so didn't go. The Captain and commandant of the camp is in bed with the "flu." Some of the boys got to feeling pretty happy at the party. They drank toasts to everyone under the sun. The camp dentist seemed to be most affected, and he is a middle-aged man too. After the party they pulled off a grease pole stunt, but it was too greasy, and no one succeeded in getting up to the top. At the top were 4 bottles of champagne, a chicken and a package containing 100 liras. When it was found out that no one could get up it, the crowd stood back, and each man got 3 shots with stones at the prizes. If a fellow broke a bottle he got a bottle of champagne, if he killed the chicken, he got it, and one fellow got the 100 liras and 16 days leave. He was a crippled fellow, and we were all glad to see him get it. Of course, the contest was for Italian soldiers only. We had heard yesterday a.m. that the different prizes were to be thrown from an airplane and let the fellows scramble for them and I think that would have been much better. Of course, champagne bottles could not have been used in that case.

Saturday, September 21st

No oil today and so no flying. I have a bad cold and cough. A couple more fellows are sick now and they called for volunteers to help in the hospitable this a.m. Of course, several fellows were willing to help. I heard today that two or three American Red Cross nurses were coming down from Rome to help out. The hospitable force is practically all under the weather. It was announced yesterday at the party that this school is to be enlarged and that new planes are on the way. We were all in hope that it would be abandoned but the government thinks that it is good propaganda whereas it is the opposite in my opinion for we do not jibe at all with the Wops. If anything, it causes ill feeling. I feel sorry for the boys that come down here and then too it means that we will have to stay here longer. With no new planes we would have gone to northern Italy for part of our training. Took a walk last night and am going to take one now. It is awfully hot and sultry today. Feels like rain.

Sunday, September 22nd

No flying today because of lack of oil. It is the same old story of Wop inefficiency. No flying for 10 days because of weather conditions; then no flying for several days because of busted planes; then an indefinite layoff because of a lack of oil. I tell you it's a terrible war. It is very plain to be seen why the Italians have not made better progress in this war. No wonder why we lose all of our pep and ambition and don't care if we never get to the front.

Monday, September 23rd

The ball team and track team came back from Rome this a.m. The ball team won 7 to 4. In the track meet the Americans won two first places and a 4th and 5th place. It was a meet between the Italians, French, English, Belgians, and Americans. I believe that the Americans finished 2nd or probably 3rd. Not bad for only having 4 men in the meet.

No flying today for there is still no oil and none in sight. Four nurses came down from Rome this a.m. There was a call for medical help from Foggia yesterday. Day before yesterday I understand that fifty-five people died in Foggia. They were dropping off like flies I am told. There is a lack of medical attention, and they are too ignorant to know how to take care of themselves. The drug stores are always crowded, and people are lined up out into the streets waiting to buy medicine. The dead have been old people and children. Two mechanics here at camp have died. I am feeling quite a bit better today. My cold and cough are much better, and my throat is not nearly so sore. To make things worse downtown the merchants raised their prices almost as much again on some articles of food and when the city authorities fixed certain prices at which they were to sell eatables the merchants got back at them by not opening their stores at all. I don't know how the matter was decided but I do know that we only had one egg apiece instead of two at breakfast this a.m. because of the efficiency in buying them. This crowd of robbers and crooks may make the food situation very bad.

Tuesday, September 24th

Still no oil and hence no flying. Vague rumors about the camp being abandoned. Fifty to sixty people are dying every day in Foggia. Six have died here so far. No Americans are dangerously sick. As for myself, I am much better. It is rumored that the Italian authorities are going to have the camp closed. Also rumored that the medical authorities (American) are to have it closed. The most pleasant but the most impossible rumor of all is that the camp is to be closed for a month or so and that quarters are to be supplied to us at a hotel in Sorrento, a fashionable resort near Naples. Not on your life, we are in the army. This lying around and doing nothing surely does get a person's nerve. If something doesn't happen soon, I will have to go A.W.O.L. and run off for a day or two to some neighboring town.

Wednesday, September 25th

As yet no oil. Have to pass the time reading and writing letters and playing cards. The Italians claim that they catch malaria and flu at night so there will be no more night flying here until the 1st of November. I understand no flying before 7 a.m. and none after 7 p.m. I presume that a man will be sent from here to another school when he gets as far as night flying. The sick are all doing nicely.

Above: SAML S.2 2044. Italy bought Aviatik biplanes prior to the war and obtained a manufacturing license. The resulting SAML series was continuously updated with more powerful engines (this one has a 300 hp FIAT) and remained the backbone of Italy's reconnaissance units throughout the war due to the robust airframe that was able to handle the rigors of frontline combat service. Italian designs intended to replace it had better performance but either had too many technical issues or were too fragile for combat.

Right: With a top speed of 147 mph, the SVA 5 was the fastest WWI aircraft to see operational service. It also had a good ceiling and excellent long-range performance, making it an excellent reconnaissance plane. Here one is photographed over the Alps by a squadron mate.

Thursday, Sept 26th

Same old story, no oil. Yesterday p.m. we all had to move out of one of our barracks and into another because some 300 Austrian prisoners are coming to this camp to do some work. Wop soldiers are moving into our barracks, and the Austrians are moving into the Wop's old quarters, so it is a grand change. Our new quarters are OK and consist of smaller rooms with from 4 to 8 men in a room. Formerly we lived in a larger room with some 25 to 30 men in it. I am rooming with 3 other boys, two of whom are from Princeton Ground School; one of them was in the same class as myself. He is a fine fellow from St. Paul, Minnesota. One of the others is from Jersey City and the 3rd is from Montana. I heard last night that 70 people had died in Foggia in the last 24 hours.

At noon today we were told that oil had come and that we would be flying this evening. Then we heard that the shock of starting to fly so quickly after so long a rest would be too much for the Wops and that we wouldn't start flying until tomorrow morning. Then about 7 p.m. we were told that the oil they had gotten was heavy oil and no good at all for motors. So, we are just as bad off as before with no oil in sight. It took over a month for us to get this oil down from Genoa so you can imagine how long we may be here doing nothing.

Friday, September 27th

Loafed all day as usual. Good reports are coming in from all battle fronts especially from Palestine and Macedonia. Heard today of the deaths of three boys that I knew. Two were flying on the front and the third was still in training. Also heard of another boy that was badly broken up in training. Several of the boys tried to get leave today but failed so I knew that there was no use of my trying. I have tried 3 times in the last six weeks and have failed. Of course, there are always the favored few who can get away almost at will while the majority of us have to stick around all the time. Five fellows left the night before last and one last night and every one of them has had bushels of leave. I have had only 3 days leave in a whole year overseas service while most of the fellows have had 3 weeks to a month leave. Some of the boys do all sorts of things such as letting on to be very sick to get away on sick leave, of course, only a few do that. Oh well I am saving money, and my chance may come someday.

Saturday, September 28th

Raining this a.m. am glad to see it for we haven't had rain for 6 weeks and everything has been dried up and it has been dry and dusty. Then too the rain will purify the air and probably break this epidemic of influenza. That is what happened up in Turin recently. Fifty-two died in Foggia yesterday. Excellent news from the fronts today. The allies have routed the Turkish army in Palestine and have taken 45,000 prisoners and a mob of guns. Bulgaria is asking for armistice because the allies have made a big drive in Macedonia and have entered Bulgaria at one point. Then the best news of all for us Americans is that the Americans are driving up in France again and have gained 9 miles and 5,000 prisoners the first day. Pennsylvania troops are taking part in this drive, so the Italian papers say. We have heard that it has rained every day for the past two weeks on the western front and of course has held the allies back. Too bad to give the Germans time to recover from their defeat.

Sunday, September 29th

No oil and so flying yet. Big British drive at Cambria reported and progressing in fine style.

Monday, September 30th

Oil arrived today but they did not get it out from the station, so we did not fly at all. Same old Italian way of putting things off.

Tuesday, October 1st

We started flying this a.m. but it commenced to rain and so it was called off. Just the luck that we should have bad weather when we have oil and are ready to fly. Paycheck today.

Wednesday, October 2nd

Windy and raining today and so no flying. I went on duty as officer of the day again today at 11 a.m. The Captain is in Rome just now on business. The epidemic of influenza in Foggia is not so bad now but we are still in quarantine and are not allowed to go downtown. The rain and cool weather have cut down the amount of sickness a lot. The death rate averaged 50 to 60 a day for several weeks in Foggia. A good-sized mail came in today. I got letters from May McQuiston, Mary Mercer, and a classmate of mine at college. May said that Art was going to take a course at Carnegie Tech. Was glad to hear that for I think that means that he will have a good chance to get a commission.

Thursday, October 3rd

I got up really early this a.m. for as officer of the day, I was responsible for having the other boys up in time to be at the hangar roll call for flying. It was very windy and so I didn't get them up until the regular hour for I knew that there would be no flying. The adjutant happened to be up and gave me a good howling out because I had not gotten the boys up earlier. I told him that I thought that there would be no flying on account of the weather conditions and he said it wasn't my place to think anything about it. He said that I should have woken the chief pilot and asked him. He told me to hurry the boys out without breakfast, which I did. I was right after all for there was no flying and so nothing further was said. It just happened that he and several others stayed up all night playing poker and drinking and that probably accounted for is his bad humor. His name is Morgan Belmont and as his name implies, he is said to be a wealthy N. Y. society man. Instances like these occur very often and show the lack of understanding between ground officers and flying officers. The trouble is that the ground officer runs the camps and lays down rules for flying, etc. when they really don't know anything about flying themselves. We had a doubles tournament here today; played it in one of the hangars on a cement court. There were 15 teams in all. My partner and I were among the last 4 teams to stay in but lost a very close set to the team which is now in the final match, and which has a good chance of winning out. We should have beaten them if we had had a little luck. Each one of us chipped in about $.75 and some small prize will be given to the winners.

Friday, October 4, 1918

Flying today and I had a good lesson. I made or tried to make 4 landings. But they weren't too successful. I seem to have quite a bit of trouble landing this machine as it is large, and I am rather small to handle it. A couple of days ago 300 Austrian prisoners were brought here to camp to do some work around the camp in cleaning up the flying field, etc. They pulled in here about 5 p.m. and were pretty shaggy looking crowd for they had not had anything to eat for 25 hours. Most of them are old peasants and have been prisoners for 2 or 3 years. They were well clothed and looked well treated for prisoners. They were given a good full-sized meal of soup, macaroni, beef, wine, and bread right away. The Italians say that they got fed better today than they themselves do. It is the policy of the allied governments to treat prisoners very well so as to encourage more and more to surrender. They are paid 11 cents per day here in Italy while the Italian soldier gets only 2 cents. It is about the same proportion in France and England too. I believe it is a good idea.

One of the boys here in camp had a letter from one of the fellows who is flying at a camp near Milan and this boy said that it was reported up there that I had been bumped off, i.e., killed. Naturally, I was very glad to be able to refute the rumor.

Saturday October 5th

Rainy weather and no flying today. Spent quite a bit of the day playing cards, reading war news, sleeping, etc. Word came in today that some eight or ten of the boys would be leaving for the front in a few days. The Lieutenant that has been in charge of flying here for about eight months and who has made this camp a success is one of those to leave. A big feed was given in his honor yesterday evening with a little wine, champagne, etc. on the side. We had a fine time and an excellent meal. This fellow is to have charge of all American fliers on the Italian front which means at least a Captaincy for him and if anyone deserves it, he does. He takes Captain LaGuardia's place as the latter is going back to the states this month for the fall elections. We were all glad to see Lieutenant Lowman (24) get the job, for he has worked hard, and he has a fine head on him and is a fellow who will give a person a square deal. The best part of it is that he has beaten Lieutenant McGilvary (23) (our old commandant at West Camp) out of the job. Nobody liked him at all, and we are all glad that he will not have a chance to give us a rotten deal. Lowman (24) gave us a very encouraging talk and said that our prospects were excellent. He said that we would go to the Italian front for a short time, probably 2 months for experience and then we would be sent to England to fly Handley-Pages and DeHavilland's. Then we would either be sent back home as instructors or to France where our job would be to bomb Metz, Cologne, and the Rhine towns. Either prospect looks especially bright to me.

Sunday October 6th

Rain again and so no flying. Am sort of glad that there is no flying for I have been sick for a day or two. I have a touch of dysentery and am now on a soft diet and take my meals at the hospital. The nurses treat a fellow fine over there. I eat a little chicken soup, rice, or drink some eggnog about 5 times a day. They dosed me with castor oil at first. I feel sort of weak. They have a case of pneumonia in the hospital. The "flu" developed into pneumonia with this boy. The epidemic is not so bad in Foggia now. The daily death rate has been reduced from 90 or so a day to about 25 or 30 a day. The epidemic is all over Europe and is quite serious in some places. Schools have been closed, also, public meetings stopped, etc. This was the case at Milan where one of our boys who went up from here a few weeks ago died of the 'flu" and the pneumonia. Coulter was his name.

Monday October 7th

Still rainy weather and no flying. I am just as glad for I am beginning to feel some better. The boys are getting pretty lively being cooped up for so long. Some of them have had pretty lively parties in the last couple of days. News from the front is excellent these days. With Bulgaria out and Turkey ready to quit and the allies driving the Germans back constantly on the western front things look pretty rosy.

Tuesday October 8th

Big news this a.m.! According to the communique received about 7 a.m. the Germans asked for an armistice to discuss peace. They want a cessation of the hostilities on land, on sea and in the air and they accept President Wilson's 14 points as a basis of the peace discussions. This is a big stride forward toward peace, but it looks like a trick to gain time for the Germans and to save them a bad beating in the field. The Italians are all excited and many of them think that the war is over and say that they expect to go home in a few days. At Milan, all work was called off and they had a big celebration, and I understand that such was the case in many places back in the states. I don't believe that anything will come of it just now for the allies are too wise. It is the most dangerous piece of propaganda the Germans have put out and if we are not pretty careful it may cause dissension among the allies.

Wednesday October 9th

Flying weather today and I had a good lesson except that I didn't do well enough to solo. I made a couple of good landings out of three, but it was too windy and bumpy to send a man up for the 1st time alone. News from the front is still very good. Another tennis tournament is on. I won my 1st game easily but was put out in the 2nd round by the winner of the other two tournaments. I had him 4-2 and 6-5 but I hadn't had enough practice and showed a lack of exercise while the other boy was in excellent condition. He beat me 8-6.

Thursday October 10th

Well at last I got off dual control. I had 4 landings with my friend the Wop instructor and only made one good landing out of four, but he turned me loose after cussing me quite a bit. I made two solo flights and laid down two good landings. The last one was perfect. Both times I pulled right up to the line and stopped, a feat which is not at all easy. He clapped his hands and said "Multo bene" (Very well) "Bravo!" He was just as profuse in praise as he had been in cussing me out. I surely was glad to have done so well just to show him that I could. He seemed quite proud of me. Heard in a letter today that a boy named Herrick (25) from Massachusetts had been killed at Issoudun. He was doing formation flying and another plane did some sort of a maneuver and cut the tail of Herrick's (25) plane right off. Too bad for he was a nice fellow and a good flier. News today that Cambrai has fallen.

Friday October 11th

Flying today but was not supposed to fly until another fellow solos so that when we are ready to brevet there will be two of us. You see the Caproni is a big plane and always has two pilots, 2 machine gunners and a mechanic when flying over the lines. In this school we take 6 rides of 15 minutes each all alone in a 300 H.P. plane and then two fellows climb to 10,000 ft or over together and make a shot at the square, i.e., landing within a certain space on the field. The last two rides constitute a brevet, so that is the reason I have to wait until another fellow solos so that we can brevet together. After the 300 brevet, we take lessons on a "450" H.P. and take a brevet and shot at the square on it. Then we do the same on a "600" H.P. plane. We also do theoretical bombing by flying over a camera obscura and flashing a light instead of dropping a bomb. We also do some regular bombing in "450" and "600" H.P. machines. Then we do night flying on both "450" and "600" H.P. planes. So, you see its quite a long course.

President Wilson's reply to Germany came out in the communiques today. He refuses an armistice or rather refuses to talk of one until the Germans get out of all invaded territory. He also asks Germany if she really accepts all his terms and asks her if he is dealing with The Kaiser or the German People. Instead of being caught in a trap he has turned the tables and has put the whole thing up to the German Chancellor. It is a clever diplomatic move, and Wilson is considered one of the greatest diplomats of all time. We are all glad to see that Wilson has gotten the better of The Kaiser.

Saturday October 12th

Columbus Day. The Italians can't understand why we fly, i.e., work on a holiday but there was flying a.m. and p.m. We had a big feed this evening consisting of turkey and dressing, green peas, potatoes, soup, salad, cake, ice cream, punch, etc. It sure was some feed. After the big meal we had speeches, music etc. and a jolly good evening. The Commandant made a little speech, also the Italian Commandant made a few appropriate remarks. One doctor has been appointed Chief of the Medical Service for Italy, and we presented him with a very fine cigarette case. He made a few appropriate remarks in acceptance.

Sunday October 13th

Well today is the anniversary of my sailing from the States, and I celebrated by taking two good solo flights, one of 25 and the other of 18 minutes. Some of the boys are a little superstitious about flying on the 13th or on Sunday, but there isn't any use of being that way when we are in this war to win. I did good work this a.m. I am due another service stripe (Chevron) for my second six months of overseas service. I presume that there are very few fellows over here now who are due second service stripes. I was among the 1st 95,000 and a lot of these boys have been killed or wounded and sent back home. I don't suppose there are over 4,000 men over here now who have been here over a year. A year is long enough, but I surely would like to get to the front before going back.

Monday October 14th

Rain and no flying today. Good news from the front. The Germans are retiring rapidly in Champagne and near Leon it was announced this a.m. in a communique that Germany has accepted all President Wilson's conditions and agrees to evacuate all occupied territory. It is now up to Wilson, and it looks as if he might have to take them at their word. He can't say that he has changed his mind and decided to ask for stricter terms. It looks as if the war might finish quickly but I hope not before I get to the front. A general order was read to the Italian soldiers today stating that this was all German propaganda and to forget it and keep at work for a few months longer and then we will get a just peace. These ignorant people want peace very badly and it might be very difficult to get them to work if this peace talk were let go unhindered.

After a month without word from home I got a letter from papa and one from mama just chuck full of news. Was sorry to hear of John Johnston's death. Have also heard that Doc Earhart died of wounds. One of the boys got a letter from France today telling of the deaths of 4 more good friends all fliers, Middlekauf (26) from Columbus, Ohio; Robertson, Forman (27) and Gustafson (28) are the others. It is too bad. I understand that only 10 men out of the company from Greensburg are in full health. Bob Woodend's company was badly busted up too, I guess. Malley (29) from Greensburg is here in camp; also, a Devoe (35) boy from Du Bois, Young from Clearfield and a couple of boys (one named Messener) from Pittsburgh.

Tuesday October 15th

I got another ride today. Did only fair. A fellow while taxiing on the ground ran into an Austrian prisoner who was working on the field and broke his collar bone and both legs. Too bad, but he is getting along O.K. in the hospital. When writing home, we kid along about flying over the Austrians daily then explain later in the letter that we are flying over prisoners. This poor fellow did not get flown over but got hit. My flying partner is Malley (29) or Haas from Greensburg. He is a fine boy but a poor flyer. He had two bad smashes at West Camp and was lucky not to have gotten killed. He did poorly at Tours too. He doesn't want to fly very badly and would like the war to end so he could quit. I will fly with him but expect to do most of the flying. He did rather poorly in his solo work on a Caproni so far.

Wednesday October 16th

We flew a while this a.m. but it was pretty rough. I got a ride and so did Malley (29). I made a perfect landing, so the instructor said. I have only two more rides before breveting now. My machine worked poorly this a.m. but I managed to stay up and do what I was supposed to. We haven't had any fatal accidents around here recently. A couple of propellers have broken in the air but due to good headwork nothing serious resulted. A motor caught on fire at 7,000 ft. the other day, but the two fellows cut off the gas and brought the plane down undamaged. They were commended for good head work and coolness in the Italian orders of the day. These planes have a bad habit of catching on fire and that is about the meanest death possible. A couple of days ago, part of a troop train was wrecked near Foggia and quite a few were hurt and about 4 or 5 killed.

The quarantine has been lifted as the "flu" has about left Foggia. I may go downtown tonight just to get away from this hole. This monotony is fierce, and I see no chance to get away on leave for some time to come. A person just almost rots down here. To see a movie show in Foggia will be a luxury. Some of the Captain's favorites can and are getting leave but I am not on the inside. My Italian instructor went on leave a couple of days ago and we made him a present of $20.00 and some cigarettes which are a luxury to Italians now. He was very well pleased.

Thursday October 17th

Up early to fly but a storm was coming up and the weather was rough, so we didn't fly. It rained most of the morning and then cleared up this p.m. but was still rather rough. I did about 40 minutes flying and finished my solo work on "300" machines. I expect to go to bed early tonight for I will have to do about 1 1/4 hours flying tomorrow to take my brevet. My partner flies with me tomorrow.

President Wilson's latest reply to Germany was published this a.m. and is another masterpiece of diplomacy. He says that the Germans must quit burning towns, sinking ships, and bombing hospitals before the allies will treat with them. He also asks for guarantees that he is dealing with the German people and not with the Kaiser and his crowd. If he is dealing with the German people all right, but if not, an unconditional surrender of the German army if the Kaiser is still king bee. Any peace or armistice has been removed quite a bit, but the way is still open if Germany wishes peace badly enough.

Friday October 18th

Raining this a.m. and so no flying. The machines were all out, but it started to rain about 7 o'clock. This is the 3rd time that has happened lately and it sure does make a fellow sore because we get up at 5:30 a.m. and then have a long day ahead of us with nothing in the world to do. If it would only start raining before 5:30 a.m. we could sleep until 7:30 a.m., which would help a lot. At 2:30 p.m., a formation was held, and each man was given a certificate for a Xmas package. We will probably all be sick from overeating for these parcels are <u>immense</u> (9X4X3 inches.) It is the best and fairest way to do it for Xmas; isn't Xmas without a package of some sort. This method will be fairer than last year when some fellows got a dozen or more packages and others got none at all. All packages have to be mailed in the states before November 20th, so it looks as if they were a little late in giving us our certificates for it is already the 18th of October and the mail is very slow just now. Hope my package gets here more quickly than last year for out of 7 packages I got 3 and these didn't arrive until the latter part of February or the 1st of March.

At this same formation, a Wop hotel clerk from Foggia was present and looked us all over. He claimed that some officer from this post had been eating regularly at his hotel and that he had borrowed a small sum of money from him and never paid it back. As you know we are not allowed to eat downtown on account of the filth. This fellow couldn't pick any of us out as being the man and so his bluff was called. He probably lied to the Captain just to try to get the Captain to pay the money. He probably thought that the Captain would pay it and say nothing about it but he was fooled fortunately.

No one thought that there would be flying this p.m. but we were called out about 4 o'clock. It was very rough and no dual control flying was done. Malley (29) and myself finished our solo work; he is getting 3 fifteen-minute rides and I two. I did particularly well on one ride and was complimented by the instructor. I am ready to brevet now.

Saturday October 19th

Weather appeared fine this a.m., but when a person got up, it was very, very rough. The chief pilot debated for some time about sending us up to do our brevet but since we had flown quite a bit in bumpy weather, he decided to start us off. I took the plane off the ground and believe me it was bumpy. Ordinarily it is bumpy up to 700 or 800 meters and then it gets smooth again but today it was bumpy clear up to 2,500 meters. We were kept busy and both of us got pretty tired. Of course we took turns driving the bus. When we were just about through the worst bumps and would have had little chance to rest up and look around a bit, the central motor went bad and the whole plane commenced to vibrate. We were at 220 meters and were required to get to 3,000 to pass the brevet test. We did our best to climb with two motors and a poor third one, but it could not be done so we piqued over and stared down mad as the d-----! because we hadn't made our altitude. As we came down, I kept trying the throttle on the central motor and every time the motor missed and shook the entire plane. However, when we got down to 1,300 meters it seemed to go OK again and so I put all 3 motors on, and we started up again. At about 2,400 meters it started to miss again and then went better again and we fought it and finally just touched 3000 meters when it got very bad, and we cut off and started for terra firma. While fooling with the motor we sort of lost track of where we were going, and a strong wind had been blowing so we found that we were about 20 miles from camp with a very strong wind against us and only two good motors. So, I used the two motors, and we slowly made headway toward home. The throttle of the central motor didn't shut off and the motor raced and shook the plane. While I had my hands full driving the bus Ed Malley (29) was more than busy with the pump. I managed to bring the bus down OK and made a fairly good landing. It sure was bumpy when we came down. All in all, we both agreed that it was the worse ride we had ever had. After having the motor fixed, we were going to go up for our shot at the square, but an air raid alarm came in and so all planes were kept on the ground. As usual no enemy planes showed up although they said that some had been sighted not far away. A couple of boys were about to brevet on a "450" when we came down but even though they had more flying time than we they were not allowed to go up on account of the bumps. The head motorista said that the central motor was not regulated for high altitudes, i.e., there wasn't the proper mixture of gas and air. He knew that we were going up for a brevet so why he didn't fix it I don't know. That is just like the Wops though. The brevet on the "300" consists of a 45-minute ride to 3,000 meters or over and of a ride to 1,200 meters from where you are supposed to cut and spiral down and make a landing in a certain space on the ground without putting on the motors again. The idea is to assume that you have to make the landing without any motors so as to give a fellow practice in judging altitude in case his motors actually do go wrong. I did excellent, cutting off at 1,400 meters and never touching the throttles and making a perfect landing at the right spot. A little flying this evening but our plane didn't work so we stayed on the ground. Malley (29) and I went to town and took in the movies this evening.

Sunday October 20th

Flying this a.m. and Malley (29) and I had a good, pleasant ride compared to what we had yesterday. Probably because it was Sunday we all had pretty poor luck this a.m. One of the instructors overshot and broke a landing gear off; machine out for days. A solo man broke elastics on landing gear; a tester took the plane that Malley (29) and I flew yesterday up to test it, and the aileron wire slipped off so that it could not be controlled from either seat. The tester said that the air was smooth as glass, and he managed to get down without smashing up. If this had happened yesterday in that bad weather neither of us would have been here to tell the tale today. But in this game, we can't afford to think of such things for if we did, we wouldn't feel like flying at all. The best thing to do is not to think about what might happen. After the wire had been put back on the pulley, we took the plane up again and had a fine ride without anything happening. Malley (29) and I did not fly this p.m. because the instructor on "450's" is sick and we are finished with "300's". Went down to town again tonight and saw the movie. Always back by 10 o'clock.

About 2 p.m. today, some 500 Italian soldiers were lined up outside and then the roll was called and each man filed past a desk where he was given a card of some sort. Some cards had a picture of General Diaz; others a map of Trentino, which Italy wants from Austria; others sample of propaganda dropped in the Italian lines by the Germans and Austrians; other samples of propaganda dropped on Vienna and among the Austrians by the Italians. Some were written in German, other in Austrian, other in Italian, Spanish, etc. I got one written in Italian and Spanish. Some of the stuff was ridiculous and would be laughed at by the Americans, French and English but to look at these ignorant soldiers, I can readily see how they and the Austrians and Russians believe such bunk.

Monday October 21st

Fine a.m. and lots of flying but my instructor an Italian is still sick, so I didn't get a ride. It has been beautiful weather with moonlight nights lately and they have been flying most nights for the last two nights. I am not feeling very well today. The dysentery has come back on me again. May have to go on a diet again. Excellent news from the front. Brugge, Zeebrugge, Ostend, etc. have fallen and a big German retreat is on in northern Belgium. Also rumored that Turkey has surrendered.

Tuesday October 22nd

Flying both a.m. and p.m. today, but due to lack of "450's, I didn't get a ride either morning or afternoon. Would like to keep going along and quit killing time. Malley (29) and I walked to West Camp for exercise this a.m. and paid a visit to the Italian commandant who is a dandy fellow and speaks good English. His name is Orlando which is a big name here in Italy. He is related to the present Italian premier. His father owns the greater part of Sicily, so I understand. He wanted us to stay for lunch, but we said that we had to get back. Talked over old times and he was very sorry to hear of the deaths of a dozen or more American he had known at West Camp. He told us of two Italian instructors who had been killed at West Camp since we left for France. The camp is quite a bit larger now, but the Captain said that there weren't many students and that the planes were no good. When I saw so many wrecks of planes, I just wondered what a bunch of junk these planes and thousands of others all over the world would be after the war. The Captain told us of the death of Lieutenant Casali in Rome last week caused by the influenza. Lieutenant Casali was an Italian count and was in charge of flying at West Camp when we were there. He spoke some English and was very funny and witty. I liked him more than other Italians I have ever met, and the other boys felt the same way. It is the irony of fate that a man should fly over the front in all sorts of danger for 2 or 3 years and not get a scratch and then just die a natural death from some slight disease. Also heard today the death of a boy named Richter (30) whom I knew. He turned down a Captaincy in the infantry for a 2nd Lieutenant in the air service. While doing formation flying at Issoudun he had the tail of his plane cut off by another machine. Tough way to die when it is not a fellows own fault.

Ten fellows left here last night for the front. Only wish that I had been going along, but perhaps I'll get there before long. A fellow only gets from 2 to 4 flights over the front a month so it is safer up there than down here flying old planes.

Wednesday October 23rd

Very foggy this a.m. and threatening rain so no flying. Ever since three fellows were killed here last fall in a collision in the fog, they are careful about flying in the fog. Germany's reply to President Wilson came out in a communique this a.m. Germany claims that she has called her submarines and ordered her generals to evacuate all occupied territory, that she has changed her government so that is more democratic. Of course, we have to swallow all of this with a grain of salt. It looks like she is quibbling too much. Hope the allies won't grant her any armistice until she is beaten to a frazzle. Austria is in very bad shape, and she is breaking up into small states while Turkey is all in. A few months will finish this affair, I think. A boy blew in from Milan today and said that he was very much surprised to see me alive and kicking, for he too had heard that I had been knocked off. I don't know how the report ever started. They thought the same thing up at the front. Received a very good letter from Virginia Pearce this a.m. She sure gives me a lot of interesting dope and I am always glad to hear from her. Her husband has gotten into aviation pretty late and instead of flying is in a concentration camp in Texas. Hard luck I'll say.

Thursday October 24th

Rain again this a.m. and so another day of idleness. I don't know what to do with myself these days because I have written to everyone I care to and even if I owed people letters it would be hard to write them for there is nothing of interest to write about. I am all fed up on reading books and magazines and am tired of playing cards so about all I can do is to read all available dope on the war and follow it very closely. Sleeping quite a bit is a favorite occupation with all of us.

Friday October 25th

Not very good weather this a.m. but there was a little flying. Our line didn't fly because we had no planes. The school is being held up because of the lack of "450's" (Caproni) and that is what I am supposed to be flying. What "450's" they have are always out of order. After many repairs they got one ready to fly this p.m., but just as it was taking off the ground one of the propellors broke and a piece went through the upper wing right close to the aileron control wire. Such a thing is very dangerous and so the pilot didn't waste much time getting back to earth. So, we didn't fly this evening either. A boy named Young from Clearfield, PA right near home got into a side ship and then into a spin and was very lucky not to be killed. He is a good flier but doesn't use his head. I guess he thinks it smart to show off. He pulled some of the same stuff the other evening and was suspended, but now he is suspended indefinitely.

Saturday October 26th

Still wet and rainy; another indoors day. We understand that about 30 new fellows will be here the 1st of the month for training. There are only about 40 of us here now. I notice that four new "600's (Caproni) and two new "450's" have just arrived. Of course, they have been used on the front and so are not brand new. We are to have an inspection of quarters this p.m. at 2 bells. The last inspection we were complimented on the appearance of our room but don't know what will be said this time. President Wilson's reply to Germany came out in the communiques this a.m. He says that if the Hohenzollerns stay in power, it means unconditional surrender but if they get out, he will offer easier terms. That is getting down to brass tacks and he has played the "German People" idea to its full extent and so has encouraged any revolution which may be on foot in Germany and Austria. We may now look for unconditional surrender, a change in government or no reply at all and fierce fighting. The last is what I think will happen. I understand that the "opera" season is to open in Foggia this evening. Since it is Saturday night, I think I will attend this grand affair.

Sunday October 27th

Fine weather this a.m. and we did some flying. Unfortunately, I didn't get to fly. Two "450's" tried to fly, but neither one was in proper shape, so we had another day on the ground. It was a week today since I have been off the ground, so I presume that I have forgotten a good deal about flying. It was too windy for flying this p.m. and a sort of wind and rainstorm is in progress tonight, so I don't look forward to flying in the a.m. I played 3 or 4 sets of tennis today for exercise. I play about once in 3 days now. A Captain and a Lieutenant. were here today to inspect the camp. The Captain went up and had a good ride in a "600" (Caproni). Pretty soft job travelling all over France and Italy and getting all sorts of mileage money and good rides in all kinds of planes. Some fellows surely do fall in soft. The show was better than I expected last night. The company is in from Venice, and they put on a good musical comedy. The music was fine with about a 20-piece orchestra. I could follow the plot fairly well but could not get all of it for it was in Italian, of course. The opera house was full and all the Italian officers from North, South and West camps were there all dressed up fit to kill with their many-colored uniforms. Our Commandant was there too. Five of us had a box. Three of us missed the truck and had to walk the 1'1/2 miles to town and it was fairly muddy. At inspection yesterday the Captain said our room was in very good shape. The inspector looked over the quarters again today. A Farman (plane) came down near camp yesterday evening and was towed in by a truck. It had a broken crankshaft. When I looked at it closely, I found that it was the plane I had made my 175-mile raid from Campo Ovest with. I am all by my lonesome at present since one roommate is in Rome having his teeth fixed, a second is at Genoa buying supplies for the Mess (he is Mess Officer) and the 3rd has just moved to a better room with a very good friend of his. I hope that the other two boys get home soon for I feel lost without them.

Monday October 28th

The rain seemed to be over this a.m., but it was awfully windy all day, so we did no flying at all. At 1 p.m. we had a lecture on night and day bombing by a second Lieutenant who has been flying with the French as an observer. He gave us some interesting dope in a general way. He told of the French plan to bomb German industrial centers along the Rhine but also said that this plan had not yet been carried out because when the Germans made their big gains last spring it was necessary to get all the available planes to the danger point to stop the drive. We are to have these lectures daily for a while now. One of the boys got news today that one of our friends named Lindsley (31) had been killed; that another had both legs broken in a crash; that a 3rd while doing formation flying had the tail of his plane cut off and only by extraordinary head work got down and got only a broken arm and minor injuries. He landed upside down however and it is a miracle how he got out alive.[11] The boys are surely being killed off rapidly. Noticed Earl Moore's [12] death in a casualty list yesterday.

Just a year ago today we put in at Belfast harbor after a very rough voyage lasting 15 days. We had gotten lost from our convoy and were lucky to get in at any port, so we thought. We cast anchor about 4 p.m. and then set out for Liverpool about 9 p.m. the same evening with an escort of two destroyers I remember well the first sight of land I got after leaving the U.S. I was sitting on the upper deck all wrapped up in blankets for as you know I was and had been in pretty bad shape for two weeks then was just beginning to recuperate. I tell you the bleak shores of old Ireland looked pretty good to me.

Tuesday October 29th

We tried to do some flying this a.m. but it was pretty windy, and we didn't fly very long. I didn't fly at all because the instructor was busy giving one fellow 11 rides. This boy seemed rather poor, but I'd guess that it was on account of the wind. I have not been inside a machine for 11 days now because of bad weather, busted planes, etc. So, you see we lose quite a bit of time in this game. The wind was too strong for flying this p.m. We had a lecture on bomb sights and their use today. Went to the opera tonight again. This show was not quite so good as the last one.

Today, a year ago, we went out into Liverpool about 6 p.m. and disembarked about 9 p.m. Two hours later we got our 1st ride in a European train with its compartments etc. We spent all night on the train and almost froze. We tried to sleep sitting up but didn't succeed very well. About 9 a.m. we reached Borden and went out to an English rest camp there.

I am Officer of the Day today; went on duty at 11 a.m. and will be through at 11 a.m. tomorrow morning. It is very cold down here at present. We all wear fleece lined flying coats all the time and hug our little oil stoves pretty closely. Being in stone barracks has its disadvantages now just as it had advantages in the hot weather.

Wednesday October 30th

I was up at 5:30 a.m. to get the boys up for flying but it was windy and started to rain about 6:30 a.m. so I let them sleep in peace. We did no flying all day for it rained nearly all day. At 7 a.m. a call came from Foggia that a Y.M.C.A. lady was at the station and wanted an automobile to bring her out to camp for she didn't care to ride in a "Carrozza", so I saw to it that a car was sent down for her. We had another lecture on bombs and bomb sights today and then Malley (29) and I had some work on the rolling carpet to prepare us for our bombing and camera obscura work. The rolling carpet consists of a cloth which runs across rollers and a fellow sits in a tower and works a bomb sight just as if we were up in a plane. The idea is to get used to the bomb sight before actually going up to use it in a machine. I was in a good game of tennis today. A Captain who has just come here for flying training and a Red Cross Captain played against a couple of us. We finally won the 1st set 12-10 and the second 6-2. It surely was good exercise. A Red Cross Major and a Captain are in camp today to arrange for the opening of a club house for officers here in camp. Smokes are to be free; tea is to be served, all sorts of reading matter, fine furniture etc. I hope that they put in a good big stove too.

The Y.M.C.A. lady arranged a little concert at the Y yesterday at 4 p.m. It was quite a bore to stick it out, but we had to do it. Our Commandant, after telling us that she had come down especially from the Italian front to sing to us and saying how much we all appreciated it, sneaked out of the back door. He didn't pay any attention to her at all and didn't even take her to either lunch or dinner but sort of left her to the care of one of the officers who was foolish enough to be roped in. He said that she was an awful bore and none of us liked her at all. She got a pretty cool reception all told. She is the wife of the American Consul at Palermo, Sicily. She is big, coarse, and unattractive and has a sort of tin-panny voice. Three Italians from Foggia helped her by playing piano and violin solos. She cordially invited us to visit them if we ever come to Palermo, but I imagine that most of the boys will steer clear of her.

A couple of days ago an offensive was started on the Italian front. It is progressing in fine shape. In six days the British, French, Italians, and Americans (1 regiment only) have pushed forward 18 or 20 miles in some places and have captured 33,000 prisoners and a lot of guns, materials etc. All is going fine, and it seems as if the Austrians are making very little resistance. It is just a matter of walking up to the boundary line, I think. I surely would like to be up there in the drive. Austria answered President Wilson's note yesterday and asks for an armistice and says she is willing to make a separate peace. She is practically out of the war as is Turkey who is actually negotiating with the allies now. It will only be a matter of days, I believe 'til both these countries will be out of it and then Germany will be beaten in a hurry if she doesn't surrender before this happens.

Thursday October 31st

Windy and rainy and no flying today. Lecture as usual at 1 p.m. Played 3 good sets of tennis. This is Hallowe'en night, but we are not celebrating at all. Last year the event was celebrated by an air raid at our rest camp near Borden, England. The fireworks made it seem more like the 4th of July than Hallowe'en. I am now entitled to wear two service stripes (Chevrons) for the day before yesterday made 1 year since I landed on foreign soil. The old rule was that foreign service dated from the date of sailing from the U.S., but it has been changed. Under the old rule, I was entitled to my 2nd service stripe on October 13th.

It doesn't make any difference to me which way they work it. I imagine than not more than 25,000 men in the A.E.F. are entitled to 2 service stripes now for I was in the 1st 100,000 and most of the first men have been killed, invalided home, sent home as instructors and the like. I heard yesterday that another fellow I knew slightly had been killed on the Western front. His name is Heyliger Church (32), and he used to play end on the field on the Yale football team. A very good friend of mine from West Camp got his 1st Hun a couple of days ago. Another fellow I know slightly has just gotten his 9th Hun. Not bad, eh what? A boy who roomed right next to me at Princeton Ground School was mentioned in the paper day before yesterday as having had a fight with a Hun but neither man won.

Friday November 1st

A strong gale blowing this a.m. so no flying. The same thing this evening. Lecture on bombing at 1 p.m. Played tennis this afternoon. One of the boys got word in a letter today that two more of our West Camp friends had been killed. Kennedy (33) and Dushek (34) were their names. This is getting quite too frequent. Austria has asked for armistice and has sent representatives into the Italian lines to talk it over. It looks like as if she is practically out of it.

Saturday November 2nd

Flying this a.m. but the 450 H.P.(Caproni) machine was not in flying condition, so I didn't get up. My partner and myself were in a plane ready for a joy ride but a mechanic found that an oil pipe on the right motor was broken and that all of the oil leaked out. So, we didn't get up. It has been two weeks to the day since I have been off the ground. A year ago, tonight we spent sleeping on the floor of a box car (22 of us to each car) and it sure was a hard bed and mighty cold. Last night a year ago we were crossing the channel from England to France and what little sleep we got was obtained under considerable difficulties. As for myself, I lay down on a wet deck with nothing but a life preserver between me and the deck. For four or five days and nights straight, we never took our clothes off at all, even sleeping in our over coats.

The Italian offensive which started the 24th of October, and which looked like a fizzle at first is progressing fine mow. In a week, the number of prisoners is about 50,000 and of captured guns 1600 and many towns have been liberated. Reported this evening that Austria had signed an armistice, but it was found to be untrue later on. Was down at the theater tonight. Fair show.

Sunday November 3rd

Flying today and I had one lesson consisting of 3 hops on a "450" (Caproni) this a.m. Due to the fact that I had not been up for 2 weeks I was pretty stale and didn't make very good landings. This p.m. we were all taking joy rides and I had a dandy with the Italian officer in charge of flying. He made a poor landing, however. About a dozen boys who left here six weeks ago for Milan to be sent to the front from there came back yesterday for further training. That is the way it goes; we had been doing our level best to get to the front for a year now, but our efforts are unavailing, and it looks now as if the war would be over soon. It is just a question of too many pilots and not nearly enough planes. Ten boys who left here 3 weeks ago for the front have gotten right into it and are helping in this big drive. Believe me, I surely would like to be up there right now. Reports this evening say that Trieste, Trento, and Udine have been taken and that the prisoners now number 100,000. It sure looks like the end of Austria. I don't know what will happen to us if Germany holds out; we will be sent either to the western front or to a new front along the southern boundary of Germany.

Monday November 4th

Good flying weather today this a.m. and Malley (29) and I did our camera obscura work which took us 1 hour and a quarter. We did good work and made some good shots even though we had trouble with the bomb sight and with one of our motors. The fellow in charge of this work here is John Devoe (35) from Du Bois, PA.[13] I drove the machine 1st while Malley (29) took 5 shots and then he drove while I took five. The idea is to give a person practice in using a bomb sight in theoretical bombing. Instead of dropping a bomb the bomber flashes a light at the time and this flash is recorded on a sheet of paper which is placed under a lens and inside of a box. The path of flight of the plane is traced on the paper too by the image of the plane through the lens. Flying was called off this p.m. because the Italians were having a "festa" or celebration because of the liberation of all Italian territory held by the Austrians. Big parade, etc. at Foggia and like celebrations all over Italy. A big offensive has been launched on the Western front again clear from Verdun to the sea. The Americans have advanced 12 miles on an 18-mile front and have taken 9,000 prisoners and many guns in the last two days. Our aviation is doing excellent work too. The Americans are holding the hardest part of the Western Front too. The Allies (French, American, Belgians and English) made quite a good advance along the Dutch border and are trying to turn the German right. All Serbia is liberated according to a late communique.

Three Y.M.C.A. girls and a man came today to give a concert at the "Y." We had a big dinner in their honor and it sure was fine. An excellent communique came in just before dinner and one of the Italian officers who speaks English well read it to us. It told about how in the past 11 days the Austrian army had been annihilated leaving 300,000 prisoners and 5,000 guns and much other material in the hands of the Allies. It said that 3 British divisions, two French divisions and one American regiment had given great assistance. It was generally supposed that there were a good many more Americans up there than that, but the ones who were there were only for propaganda purposes. The Italian army, of course, won the victory but in my opinion, President Wilson won 4/5ths of it with his wonderful diplomacy which broke Austria all up and caused so much internal dissention as it is doing in Germany too. The Austrians didn't fight but ran as fast as possible. Toasts were drunk to Italy, then to America and to the Allies and there were loud shouts of "Viva L'Italia!," "Viva L'America!" etc. and the spirit shown was excellent. Right after the big meal the "Y" people entertained us for a solid two hours. Miss Sue Wilson sung very well; Miss Whittlemore proved to be an excellent violinist; the elocutionist was very good too, as was the pianist but I have forgotten their names. It was all a great treat for us. Some of the music was Italian in honor of about a dozen Italian officers who were our guests. There was a little dancing after the performance, i.e., cut-in-dancing, but there were so many of us and only 3 of the girls, that only a few of us danced. For some reason I was not feeling very well all day yesterday, so I came home and went to bed. I had a pain in my back; I guess a cold had settled in my kidneys.

Tuesday November 5th

Misty and foggy all day so no flying. Good news of yesterday evening from Italian front officially confirmed today and the Armistice with Austria was signed yesterday at 3 p.m. so Germany is all alone. It is and will be hard to keep these fellows at work for they feel that their war is over. The Allies have helped them, but they don't feel like returning the compliment. They were lined up and given a talking to today and they will be kept in line all right.

Wednesday November 6th

Too cloudy today for flying. Several attempts were made to fly but the clouds were too low. I spent most of my time this a.m. running back and forward between the barracks and the flying field because several times they tried to fly and so called us all out and then we came back again right away. I translated President Wilson's latest reply to Germany this a.m. and put on the "Y" bulletin board. He says that the Allies are willing to treaty with the Germans for he had been informed by the Allied Council at Versailles. All the conditions he had previously laid down would stand and the communique stated further that Marshall Foch had been authorized to carry on the negotiations. Another report came into the effect that German representatives had left Berlin yesterday to come to the Western Front to discuss the terms of an Armistice. Believe me they didn't waste much time after President

Wilson told them that Foch would talk to them. They seem pretty anxious to quit. In the meantime, the Allies are hitting the line hard clear from Metz to the sea. The Americans are doing especially good work north of Verdun. They have the toughest sector of the whole front but have advanced 12 miles on an 18-mile front in 3 days and are menacing Sedan and Luezieres. This is the strongest point of the German line and is the pivotal position. If the Americans succeed in advancing a little further the Germans will have to retreat rapidly or run the risk of having their front broken through.

Thursday November 7th

No flying this a.m. but I flew this p.m. and made 3 very good landings dual control (450 H.P. Caproni). The instructor said, "very well" (in Italian) each time and then sent me solo. I made a very good landing for which he complimented me, So I am now ready to brevet on a 450. The Allies terms of Armistice to Austria were published today and they amount to unconditional surrender. Score up a big victory for President Wilson. The Italians seem to think that the war is over, at least for them. They have gotten what they want and don't seem to care whether France wins over Germany or not. They seem to forget that the French and English helped them out and saved them from complete defeat last fall when the Austrians captured 200,000 Italians and 2,500 cannon. To keep them in line here we all have to stand roll call at 7 a.m. and 1 p.m. to make them think that we are taking more interest in flying. It is the only way to impress people as ignorant as they are. Propaganda must be used on them. The old fellow who has been making my bed, etc., is among the lucky fellows. The Austrian prisoners even look happier since Austria has been beaten. They didn't know what they were fighting for, and they realize now that Germany was an enemy not a friend of the Austrian people. They are to be pitied.

Friday November 8th

Too cloudy for brevet today. Only dual control flying at low altitudes. Very good news from France; Americans have taken Sedan and so cut off one of the two main lines of German retreat. This victory has also caused the Germans to retreat on a wide front for a distance of many miles. All the British and French have to do is hurry up by using cavalry and automobiles to keep up with the Germans. The Pennsylvania Regiment has been cited twice by General Headquarters' and our flyers are doing wonderful work having brought down 185 planes in 10 days. A good college friend of mine named Potter was brought down the other day, but it is thought that he landed safely and was taken prisoner. He has won the Croix de Guerre and the D.S.C. (Distinguished Service Cross) Another boy who was in my class at Ground School brought a plane down a few days ago. His name is A.P. Schenk [14] from Montclair, N.J. We had word from some of the boys on the Italian front this a.m. and they say that the plans are for them to bomb German towns including Berlin from there. Hope Germany lasts a little longer so I can get in on that.

Saturday November 9th

Clouds low again today and so impossible to take a brevet. Played 3 or 4 sets of tennis. Still good news from the Western front. The American victory is considered one of the biggest victories of the war. All the papers are talking about it. News came in today that the terms of the Armistice had been communicated to the German representatives by Foch. They have until Monday the 11th at noon to reply. If they say "Yes" it is unconditional surrender and if they say "No" it will be a short time until they are badly beaten up.

Sunday November 10th

Still too windy and cloudy to get up to my altitude. I am getting mighty tired waiting to do a brevet; for once I get finished up, I can get a leave. News came in this a.m. that the Kaiser had abdicated as a result of an ultimatum sent to the Chancellor saying that the Kaiser must abdicate and that the Crown Prince must renounce his claim to the throne by noon of the 9th or the Socialists would break with the government and withdraw their members from the Reichstag. So, it would seem that the Socialists have quite a bit of power for the Kaiser has yielded to their demands. Then again Erzberger, one of the biggest Socialists in Germany is on the commission, which is conferring with General Foch and too, Max Von Baden has resigned, and it is likely that Scheiderman another big Socialist is likely to succeed him. So, I think that Germany will accept any terms offered her. Germany and Switzerland have both broken off relations with Russia because Russian Socialism is spreading over Germany, Austria, and other countries. Germany's own propaganda is coming back on her and President Wilson's propaganda is doing wonders. The war has been largely won for us and lost to Germany by propaganda. In a letter from France we heard today Pichon, All-American quarterback from Dartmouth and whom we knew very well at West Camp had been killed while ferrying a plane. Also, another good flier from West Camp, Malcolm has been killed at the front. Deaths are thick and fast in aviation. R.W. Wright another friend was brought down in our own lines but not killed. A 4th West Camper landed at a German aerodrome, discovered his mistake, and got away OK. (Bailey, John W.) I expect to go downtown tonight with an Italian Officer to meet a nice Italian family. In my 8 months stay at Foggia, I have as yet met no nice Italians. They are not very sociable. If I had spent that much time any place in France, I would have known a lot of fine people.

Monday November 11th

Armistice signed. War over. The Kaiser and Crown Prince have fled to Holland. News that we are to go to France in a few days. So will terminate this diary here as I will get home to tell my story.

November 11th – 17th

Waiting to be sent to France. Several little parties at Foggia and with Italian officers at camp. We were given the right to wear the Italian Eagles and the Italian Service stripe. Flying was called off November 11th.

November 17th – 24th

En route to France. Left Foggia at 1.30 a.m. on November 18th. Sat up all night and got to Rome at 12 midnight. Did shopping etc. and left Rome at 8.30 p.m. for Florence, arriving there at 3 a.m. and going right to bed. All the other boys went on to Paris. I was A.W.O.L. for 2 days in Florence for I had been refused permission by the Captain at Foggia and the Major at Rome to stay over. Was induced to stay over by two Vice Consuls who showed me a wonderful time. I met the Consul, and quite a number of the royalty of Florence, Mr. Thompson, and others. Bought some lace, cameos, etc. Left Florence at 8 p.m. and on November 20th spent the night at Pisa and left Pisa at 5:30 a.m. on November 21st. Passed through Genoa and Turin, got supper at Modane and left there at 9 p.m. for Paris. Got to Paris at 10.30 a.m. on November 22nd. Stayed until 8 a.m. on November 23rd and did quite a bit of official business. Saw many college and army friends at the University Union and took in the Follies that night. Arrived at Poitiers at 2 p.m. on November 23rd and came to St Maxient by auto arriving at 5:30in. Reported in at 11 a.m. on November 24th and got called down because I was the last man to get in. A certificate from an Italian doctor helped me out, however.

November 24th - December 2nd

Awaiting orders to sail. Tried to get a 7 day leave but it was impossible. 35 men left December 1st for the U.S. I expect to go in a day or two. Although prohibited, I am living out in town and have a good comfortable room with fireplace and have breakfast served in bed every day. I report for two formations daily, 9.00 a.m. and 1.30 p.m., just to let them know that I am still around. That is all I do. Hard life, eh what?

December 2nd - December 14th

Still awaiting orders for the States. December 5th practically all of my friends who came up from Italy with me left for Bordeaux and sailed for the U.S. If I had not stopped over in Florence, I would have gone with them and so have been home for Xmas. I surely was mad at myself for that. It is now too late and so I have asked for permission to go to see the Freslon's and so am leaving this evening for 3 days.

December 14th – December 20th

Got to Paris the morning of December 14th (Sunday) and saw President Wilson and party come from church. He looked better than when I last saw him in the states. All the French people seem mighty enthusiastic about him and surely did give him a big reception. Had a big argument with an American woman who had lived in Paris 18 years. She was bitter against President Wilson, and I upheld him. Fortunately for me she was nearly arrested by a Secret Service man for what she said and as an army officer, President Wilson is my Commander-in-Chief. I will never forget the celebration on the Blvd. Des Italiennes that evening. There was an awful crowd, and it was impossible for taxis to get through. Everybody kissed and hugged everybody else and since the Fete was in honor of President Wilson and all the Americans who hadn't enough foresight to put their hats in their pockets had them taken as souvenirs. Leaving Paris, I went to Reuilly and spent 3 very pleasant days in the Freslon home. Mr. Freslon (Captain), being over 50 years of age, was already demobilized and we had some long talks about the war. He gave me some fine souvenirs. I gave Odette a very nice pearl ring and Paulette a necklace and Mr. Freslon a lot of tobacco and cigarettes for Xmas. Returned by way of Paris and saw a good show and got back a day late and almost got court-martialed.

December 20th – December 25th

Awaiting orders. Having an excellent time doing nothing. Nearly every evening, I visit a French family from 8:30 to 11.30 and we play "500" and have some music. The family name is Hugeneau, and they have two little girls of 15 years and the other of 8. Then a friend of the family, Madeline Guese, 26years old, is a fine girl but at present is in mourning on account of the death of her mother. She died of the "Flu." So, Madeline never goes out at all in company. I also know a family named Goudeau and one named Blanchard and I go there at times. I am learning French fast and also some slang. Herbert Long, a good friend of mine at Princeton Ground School, knows the Hugeneaus well for he was here for 4 months last winter as a cadet. So, he came to visit them the other day and I took dinner along with him twice at their home. He didn't make good as a flyer and so has been at Brest for some time. His home is in Baltimore.

December 25th – December 28th

En route to Angers which is nearer the ocean. Left St. Maixent at 7:30 p.m. Xmas evening. Xmas Eve the French go to mass at midnight and then come home to dance and eat until about 4 or 5 a.m. but I was very wise and went to bed at 10:30. Xmas night I spent at Tours, the next night at Vierzon, where I met the Freslons. The next day Odette and her cousin came as far as Paris with me, and we had a good dinner together and went to a matinee. Then they came as far as Orleans with me, and I bid them goodbye there. Arrived in Angers at 2:30 a.m. on December 27th and had a terrible time finding a hotel.

December 28th – January 20th,

At Casual Officers Camp, Angers with 1,500 other casuals awaiting orders for the states. Two formations daily, 9 a.m. and 4:30 p.m., but I know the Lieutenant in charge of my company and whether I am there or not is immaterial. So, I live in town practically all the time and have a good room and bed. Angers is a town of 125,000 and has 4 good movies and a good theatre. At camp we are not treated very well as officers. At times the camp is closed, and we can't even go downtown, I have become disgusted waiting orders and so have applied to stay in France for some time so as to learn French better for it will be very useful in business after the war. My orders came the 20th of January and so I will stay in France.

Notes:

1. Robert P Albergotti from Orangeburg, SC. Sailed on Adriatic 8 Dec 1917.
2. Ernest F Caldwell
3. Paul Daniel Nelson, PU 1917. Attended ground school at Princeton.
4. Linus V Windnagle
5. Heywood Holden, Yale. From New Rochelle, NY
6. Richard Aldworth, Princeton graduate and later with the 213th Aero Squadron.
7. Meyer Greenbaum and Phil Kissam played right field for Camp Ouest in the game.
8. Hobart AH Baker, Princeton '14 and later CO of the 141st Aero Squadron,
9. Austin Jesse Miller from Millerton, Pennsylvania as does the Passenger Manifest for his return home in 1919.
10. Carl Kohlmayer - 5 July 1918 – TOURS. Reported as killed on 5 July in the weekly casualty lists.
11. Julian N. Dowell. Princeton 1916.
12. George D. Lancaster – Discovered his hometown through passenger manifests – Ashland, Va.
13. Benjiman P Bradford, Bowdoin College class of 1917.
14. Clinton Sutton killed in a crash at Issoudun on 16 August 1918.
15. Mark Fayette Hamilton. Crashed on 3 August, died in hospital on 5 August.
16. Edgar Booth Schreiber killed on 8 August 1918
17. Arthur "Dutch" Preyer – Killed at Issoudun 31 August 1918
18. William T Gould from New York. Attended Virginia Military Institute, later 93rd Aero.
19. Harry B. Moses – Texas.
20. Donat J. Pepin
21. Donald E Yund – He survived and passed away in 1966.According to his gravestone and his draft GA records, he was from Indiana. May have enlisted in Columbus, OH.
22. David Irving Reynolds, East Orange NJ. Killed with Lt. Avogli Trotti on 9 September.
23. Eaton McGilvary from Madison, Wisc.
24. John W. Lowman, Cleveland OH
25. William B Herrick. Killed in a mid-air doing formation work with Lt. Sylvester B. Moore.
26. Mark Humbert Middlekauf, killed 15 September 1918. Does not appear on any published Foggia roster but was obviously assigned there.
27. Horace Baker Forman from Maryland, killed at Issoudun on 14 September 1918.
28. Check Gustafson – was killed at 2nd CAS.
29. Edward Michael Malley was from Greensburg, Pennsylvania and enlisted on May 11, 1917. He went to the Ohio State University Ground School and sailed to Europe on October 18, 1917. He arrived back in Foggia in August 1918 for additional training until the armistice.
30. Edward "Pops" Richter. Killed in a DH-4 mid-air at Issoudun.
31. Paul Lindsley from Colorado, Killed 5 October 1918.
32. Heyliger Church, 95th Aero, Yale 1917.
33. Alvin Kennedy killed 12 Oct at Aerial Gunnery School at Cazeaux.
34. Vincent Dushek killed 16 October 1918 at Issoudun.
35. John Devoe, Penn State U 1916.

Above: Macchi L.3 4842 at the Sant'Andrea Naval Station in Venice. Italy has extensive shorelines so seaplanes formed a significant part of her air service. Flying boats were more popular than floatplanes. The L.3 was a two-seater used for patrol, reconnaissance, and light bombing.

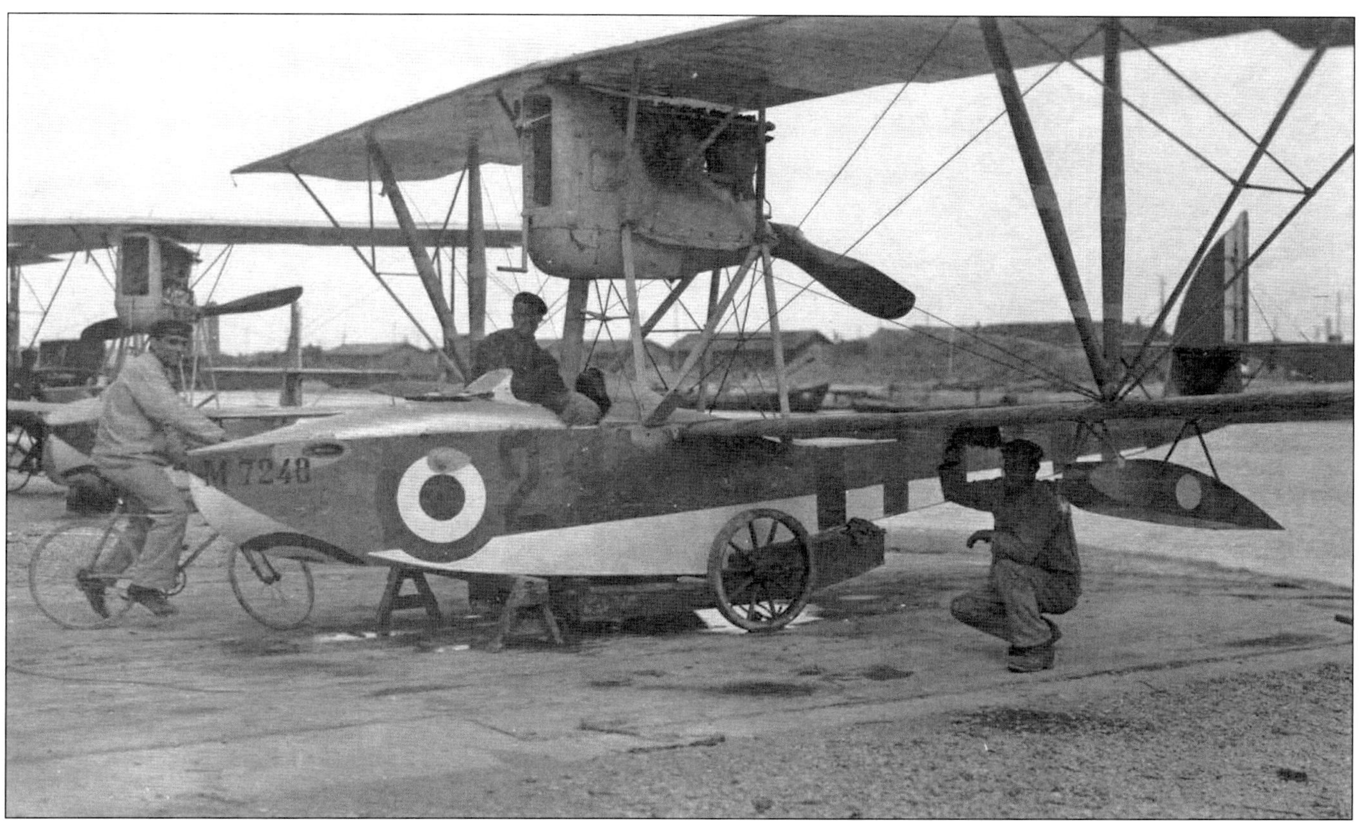

Above: Macchi M.5 M 7248 on its beaching dolley. The M.5 was the best flying boat fighter to see combat during WWI.

1919

January 20th – February 5th

Now stationed 10 miles out of Angers in a small town of 700 people. I have 4 like towns to look after. In these 4 towns 1,000 to 1,200 soldiers and officers are billeted. It is my job to see that all billets are kept in shape, that beds, stoves, and latrines are supplied to the men, to see that the French people are paid regularly for their billets and when the troops leave to settle claims made versus them by the French. This is a dirty job and especially here for the deadhead of an officer who has been here before me and has left everything pile up for 7 months. The troops left the 27th of January and so I am now busy wrangling with the ignorant French peasants. Everybody thinks the American government is rich, so everyone asks too much by 4 or 5 times. I have to call most of them thieves and liars. I have claims for everything; from 3 francs for one broken stone up to 1,400 francs for repairing a bowling alley. It surely is a dirty job, but I am learning French. I have a sidecar and driver and 3 carpenters working for me. I live with a French doctor who is much like an American and I have a spotless room with a good open fireplace. At times I spend the night in Angers after going to the theater or the like. Saw Faust (German legend) some days ago. At present, we have a little snow but for about a week it has been cold and clear. Before that, it rained every day for 3 weeks.

This is the last entry of Stewart's diary. His last duty assignment was the officer in charge of Rents, Registrations and Claims, Company #13 (his lucky number) at Angers and Paris from December 1918 to October 1919. The delay in Stewart receiving his first and second brevets and commission and aviator wings was the result of several circumstances and unfortunately did not allow him to participate fully in the war. The progression of the training for him was terribly slow and was made more so due to the lack of machines, fuel, accidents, weather conditions, insects, pandemics, health problems, poor instruction, etc.

But his story continues with his relationship with Odette and his journey and careers after the war.

Samuel Stewart's Military Summary

- Enlisted in ROTC 14 May 1917.
- Attended OTC at Ft. Myer with 5th Provisional Training Regiment until August 4, 1917.
- Enlisted in Signal Enlisted Reserve Corps (Air Service) August 15, 1917.
- Attended Ground School at School of Military Aeronautics at Princeton from August 4, 1917, to September 29, 1917. Graduated with honors.
- Transferred to Ft. Wood to await overseas Transport October 6, 1917.
- Sailed aboard SS Pannonia October 13, 1917
- Arrived at 3rd AIC, Issoudun November 5, 1917.
- Transferred to 8th AIC, Foggia February 8, 1918.
- Commissioned as a 1st Lieutenant May 13, 1918
- Transferred to Air Service Reserve Concentration Barracks at St.Maxient, France June 6, 1918.
- Assigned to 1111th Aero Replacement Squadron at Torino, Italy August 1918.
- Trained at Tours, France and Foggia, Italy February 11, 1918, to November 1918. (1)
- 2nd AIC St. Maxient, November - December 1918. (2)
- Rents, Registrations and Claims, Company #13 at Angers and Paris, France December 1918 to October 1919.
- Casual Company Brest, France September 1919
- Sailed home October 5, 1919, aboard SS Princess Matoika.
- Discharged from the Army October 27, 1919

Source was from Princeton University in the World War; St. Maxient and 2nd AIC were two different organizations-Tours training and St. Maxient was a concentration depot for personnel awaiting assignment.

NO. 16.)

9. Under authority contained in Indorsement from Headquarters, S.O.S., on letter from these Headquarters, dated January 4th 1919, the following named officers are relieved from assignment and further duty with their present organizations and will report at once to the Commanding Officer, U.S. Troops, Angers, for assignment to duty:-

Captain George I. Amos, 64th C.A.C.

1st Lieut. George M. Fields, 335th Machine Gun Battalion.

1st Lieut. James D. West, 64th C.A.C.

1st Lieut. Charles I. Clark, C.A.C.

1st Lieut. Herbert C. Bartlett, C.A.C.

1st Lieut. Willis B. Smith, 54th C.A.C.

1st Lieut. Samuel S. Robinson, A.S.

1st Lieut. George D. Lancaster, A.S.

2nd Lieut. Philip D. Shea, 64th C.A.C.

2nd Lieut. William J. Helmer, 64th C.A.C.

2nd Lieut. Alfred E. Reeves, 54th C.A.C.

2nd Lieut. Paul C. Klyce, F.A., 54th C.A.C.

2nd Lieut. Francis C. Warren, 54th C.A.C.

2nd Lieut. Cyril J. Wertz, 54th C.A.C.

2nd Lieut. Curtis F. Clauson, 54th C.A.C.

2nd Lieut. Lawrence R. Atwood, 54th C.A.C.

2nd Lieut. John H. Kern, 54th C.A.C.

2nd Lieut. Robert M. Henry, F.A., 54th C.A.C.

2nd Lieut. F.A. Birmingham, 54th C.A.C.

By order of Colonel Wright.

L. D. Bogan,
Capt. Inf.,
Adjutant.

adc-

Copies to-
BS 1
Organizations.

Military Orders to Report to Angers

A Love Story Too

Stewart received his orders to report to St. Maixent in France to ship out to the United States. He left Foggia on November 18, 1918, after the German armistice and headed to France. As he details in his journal entry, he travelled to St. Maixent on a more circuitous and adventurous route through Italy and France, and finally in late November, he made it to the St. Maixent Army Camp in France but was considered A.W.O.L. since he reported in late and therefore missed his chance to be home for Christmas.

Looking back, it was a turbulent and worrying time in Europe. Every country had been hosting four or five other countrymen speaking four or five different languages. Europe had been at war for almost three years and finally the Americans had come over to join the Allies. The Europeans were depressed, and food was scarce. All the young men were active in the war, thousands were dead, and the everyday land work was left to the elderly, women, or disabled military. They did the farming, building, merchandising, legal, medical and every other type of work that had to be done. The only men available were over fifty years of age and therefore no longer eligible to be drafted into serving their country as military men. Some had already served, and many were disabled because of it by injury, amputation, the effects of Mustard Gas and undiagnosed PTSD.

For the young girls it was a time far different than they had imagined for their teens. This was an age of deprivation and unfulfilled dreams with no young men to flatter and court them. Many young French women were drawn to the U.S. soldiers encamped near their homes. The "Yanques" were in better spirits and had endless supplies of money, candy, gum, and cigarettes. There was always a wedding between an American aviator and a young French woman once he receives his commission.

Stewart was among the second fifty American aviation cadets to be stationed at Issoudun, France in January and early February 1918. While stationed there he had visited the village of Reuilly, France many, many times before leaving for Italy. He would walk from Issoudun to Reuilly, which is approximately eleven miles, to have dinner with Odette and her family at their home or at her aunt's home. He would bring candy and cakes and other foods, and her family would provide the rest for the dinners. Every time he had to kiss Odette goodbye it had to be in front of her family. He was always breaking quarantine and being A.W.O.L. for his trips to Reuilly. Her family was affluent, and Odette had been educated in Paris for the past five years. Soon after Stewart and Odette started courting. She was nineteen, he was twenty two. Odette would call him by his first name, Samuel. Her letters to him were always addressed as "Dear Samuel." Stewart was keen to learn French to help him in business when he returned to the United States after the war, so he actively sought French people to help him. He was first acquainted with Odette's Mother, who was happy to make friends with the handsome, young, educated American and invited him to join the family for supper. Odette's father was still an active serving member of the French military at the time The fact that they had an attractive, appropriate daughter was just a lucky happenstance. At these suppers Samuel was introduced to Odette and her sister Paulette, along with Odette's Grandfather. Stewart was an erudite and charming young man who was readily approved by "Madame" and "Granpere" and became a frequent guest for an evening in the company of the whole family. Every time Samuel came to supper, he brought small gifts of chocolate for "Madame" and tobacco for "Granpere." Whenever Stewart and Odette went anywhere, they were always accompanied by a chaperone. She and either her mother, sister, or cousin, would meet Stewart in the town or walk to town after supper and Stewart treated them to many little trinkets and excursions. The young group would meet in Reuilly, France to "Promenade," a light yet romantic evening walk and then Samuel would accompany the young women home at ten or eleven o'clock. Stewart was an American aviator, both unknown and attractive to Odette and she and her mother readily encouraged Stewart's advances and their burgeoning friendship. Despite the restrictions associated with being in the military, Stewart and Odette continued to see each other whenever they could. Over the course of the year, they would manage to slip away for an evening and the occasional overnight or weekend excursion to Paris or Vierzon. Maybe they fell in love? They enjoyed each other's company, and Odette's family approved and were grateful for gifts that Stewart bought for them. At the end of the summer and early autumn of 1918, Stewart's military duties increased, and Stewart and Odette's romance was "put on the back burner".

Because of Stewart's hectic schedule to obtain his

Sheet No. 2

1st. Class

PASSENGER LIST OF ORGANIZATIONS AND CASUALS

RETURNING TO THE UNITED STATES

INSTRUCTIONS

Separate lists of TWELVE COPIES EACH will be accomplished by each company or detachment commander as follows:

1st Class: Officers arranged according to Rank, Nurses, Army Field Clerks, Field Clerks Q. M. C., Civilian Employees. Names to be numbered consecutively beginning with No. 1.

2nd Class: Non-commissioned Officers down to and including Color Sergeant (See A. R. Par. 9).

3rd Class: All enlisted men below Color Sergeant (A. R., Par. 9), arranged according to usual formation of the Company, that is, BY SQUADS.

This form when used to list CASUAL military passengers will be accomplished in like manner, but within each class all casuals will be sub-grouped under the following headings with reference to the reason for their return, not more than one such sub-group being listed on the same sheet: (1) Deceased, (2) Sick and Wounded (3) Prisoners, (4) For Duty, (5) On Leave or Furlough, (6) Miscellaneous. The word "Casuals" and the name of the group will be entered in the space provided for name of organization, and the Embarkation Personnel Adjutant will sign his name in the space provided for the signature of organization commander.

To be filled in by company or detachment commander	Give full name of organization including company and regimental designation	BREST CASUAL COMPANY 5244		To be filled in by Debarkation Personnel Adjutant, U. S. A.	
To be filled in by Embarkation Personnel Adjutant, A. E. F.	Name of vessel	Port of sailing	Date of sailing	Port of Arrival	Date of Arrival
		BREST, FRANCE			

MATOIKA

TO CAMP MERRITT

HOBOKEN OCT. 1919

No.	NAME AND SERIAL NUMBER Example: HENDERSON, HARRIS F. 1234567	Rank & Arm or Staff Corps. Example Capt. A. G.	Organization (regiment and company or detachment)	NOTIFY IN CASE OF EMERGENCY. (Give name in full, for example; Mrs. Mary A. Smith.)	Relationship Example: Foster-mother	ADDRESS (Number, Street, City and State) Do not abbreviate.
	Leave double space between entries. All typewriting must be in CAPITAL LETTERS.					
1	MOSHER, RALPH H.	CAPT. A.S.	AM. RELIEF ADSM	MRS. ELLEN P. MOSHER	MOTHER	31 EMUSON STREET MEDFORD, MASSACHUSETTS
2	CRANE, DONALD F.	1LT. 2ND F.A.	AM. RELIEF ADMS.	MRS. GERTRUDE F. CRANE	MOTHER	NO. 112 DECATUR STREET, BROOKLYN, NEW YORK.
3	ROBINSON, SAMUEL S.	1LT. A.S.	R.R.&C. SERVICE	MR. JAMES W. ROBINSON	FATHER	SALTSBURG, PENNSYLVANIA.
4						

Matoika Passenger List

brevets and wings before the end of the war, he had little time to write letters. The last entry in his journal that he made about writing letters was on October 24, 1918. This corresponds to the last letter that Stewart wrote to Odette according to Odette's letter dated December 1st. Odette's letter states that she is very sad because she has not heard from him "in 23 days" and that she hopes that he will come to France to see her and that she is thinking of him.

Odette, of course, still saw her friends from her village, girls, and boys, she had grown up with, gone to school with and befriended for years when Stewart was not around.

Since she had not heard from him, Odette thought that he had already left France, since he had not responded to her letters, until he suddenly showed up at her parents' home in Reuilly, France on December 17th to celebrate the Christmas holiday with the Odette and her family. He spent the next three days at her parent's home and presented Odette with a pearl ring and her father and grandfather tobacco and cigarettes and her sister Paulette a necklace. On December 20th, he returned to the St. Maixent Army Camp.

On Christmas day, he left St. Maixent and arrived in Angers, France, his new station, awaiting duty assignment. The next day he met Odette and her family at Vierzon, France. On December 27th, Stewart and Odette and her cousin travelled to Paris and then just Stewart and Odette travelled to Orleans, France. The next day, Odette went home to Reuilly and Stewart travelled to Angers. While he was in Angers still awaiting orders, he made the decision to stay in France longer. His justification was to learn to speak French better because it would "be useful in business." But Odette was an alluring reason too.

Stewart's new assignment as the Rents, Registrations and Claims officer in Angers, France was made official on January 15th, 1919, and he received his orders on January 20th. This duty assignment would give him plenty of opportunities to visit Odette. The distance between Angers and Reuilly, France was approximately one hundred fifty miles or about a two-hour train ride, which either Stewart or Odette could have easily done.

Soon after, Odette would discover that she was pregnant. She probably was not the first girl in her village that this happened to and, taking advice from her friends, Odette travelled over two hours by train to see a doctor in Navarre on the Spanish border. Upon learning of her pregnancy, her parents would not allow Stewart to visit her. Her affluent and strict French Catholic parents sent her away to a convent called the Cordeliers, run by the Franciscan order, in a town called Chateauroux, which was approximately fifty four kilometers from her hometown. There she lived and worked in an old convent, a home for unwed mothers. She would deliver the baby and give it up for adoption in September 1919. She returned to Reuilly at the end of September with no baby. The nuns would have cared for Odette throughout the pregnancy and then arranged for the baby to be adopted. This absence seems to have been the end of the romance between Odette and Stewart. This is atypical for this era and especially in the small town of Reuilly where everyone knew Stewart.

There was no mention of any further visits to Odette or visits by Odette nor any more letters received between December 28th, 1918, and September 29th, 1919.

Since Stewart and Odette had not communicated for nine months, Odette wrote her final letter on September 29th, 1919.

The following is the translated version of Odette's letter:

Reuilly 9-29-19

Dear Samuel

I just arrived this instant from Châteauroux. Always with terrible weather. It was necessary to go there. Because it is not a pleasure for me because since yesterday it is impossible to do much movements. I made an effort to recover and this evening I saw the doctor who advises me to stay in bed for two days. Also, this does not make me happy. My Uncle left you the package (_____) he wrote to me, but never met you.

I hope that your health is better than mine.

Tell of your news. The best kisses/hugs from your little.

Odette

Odette would move on quickly and marry a Frenchman named Edward Albert Loyer on December 19, 1919. She passed away on September 8, 1976, in Haute-Isle, Val-D'Oise, France.

Since the time that Stewart mentioned Odette in his diary entries in mid-January 1918, he never mentioned her full name. It was not until the December 2nd and 14th, 1918 diary entries that Stewart finally reveals her full name: Odette Leontine Juliette Freslon. She lived with her parents and was born on October 3, 1898. When she met Stewart in 1918, she was nineteen years old and her sister, Paulette (who also wrote to Stewart) would have been thirteen years old at the time. Her

Above: USS *Princess Matoika.*

parents were Albert and Charlotte Freslon. (Stewart did mention in one of his last diary entries that her father was a Captain in the French military.)

Stewart was disappointed by these events and was not able to visit Odette during her pregnancy. He soon met another woman while living in a small village outside of Angers and began having a relationship with a lady named Emmanuel. But this did not work out either. In May 1919, Emmanual wrote Stewart a farewell letter.

Stewart remained in Europe until September 1919. He would leave from the port of Brest, France on October 5 aboard the USS *Princess Matoika* along with three other officers and would arrive in Hoboken, N.J. on October 15th and report to Camp Merit and would be honorably discharged from the military on October 27, 1919.

This would be one of the last transports leaving from this Naval Operating Base. In September 1919, both the Naval Port Office and the Army Transport Service in Brest were ordered closed.

Stewart was deeply affected by all these events and after he finally returned to the US, lead a disrupted life, trying many professions and living in many locations before eventually settling back in his hometown of Saltsburg, Pennsylvania and marrying, at the age of fifty-nine.

Life After the War

Above: Samuel Stewart Robinson.

Samuel Stewart Robinson lived most of his life in his hometown of Saltsburg, Pennsylvania, but he did like to be adventurous and lived in Tulsa, Oklahoma, Coral Gables, Florida and Baltimore, Maryland. He worked as an insurance agent, an automobile dealer, and a banker during his lifetime.

After graduating from Princeton, he went to Baltimore and worked as a banker with Alexander Brown & Sons from 1916 to 1917. Once discharged from the Army, Stewart returned home to Saltsburg, Pennsylvania. In 1920, he visited his long-time schoolmate Virginia Pearce in Tulsa, Oklahoma. Virginia and Stewart were classmates and friends since their early school years and in the original journal Stewart writes "that Virginia should read the diaries if she wants to." While there he worked with her father at the Pearce, Porter & Martin Insurance Agency selling for the Aetna Casualty & Surety Company starting in 1920. He was hoping to rekindle a high school romance with her, but that was not in the cards. Stewart would bounce around in jobs and locations until finally returning home in 1926.

On May 2, 1925, James W. Robinson & Sons opened the Robinson Garage and began selling Dodge automobiles and trucks. But James needed someone to run the automobile business and wanted Stewart to do it, but Stewart was not ready to return home.

Then in July 1925, Stewart drove in a car for two days to Saltsburg, Pennsylvania, covering about seven hundred miles to attend a Friday night dinner and reunion of family members at his parents' home. It had been many years since the family had been together. At the dinner were his aunts Mary Mercer, Anna Robinson, his uncle's Frank, William E. and his father James W. and his mother and siblings. There is no doubt that the conversation came around to automobiles since his uncle William was the first in the county to own and drive an automobile just a few years prior. Both his father and his uncle were successful entrepreneurs and businesspeople. His father owned a funeral home, a home furnishings store that sold steam washers and refrigerators and porch furniture. His uncle owned and operated a large general store in Nowrytown, Pennsylvania, located approximately five miles from Saltsburg. Stewart's brothers were part owners of the funeral home. The seed was planted that weekend for Stewart to operate the first automobile dealership in town.

In early 1926 he was living in Coral Gables, Florida and was working in real estate there. But, then in late 1926, Stewart returned home to Saltsburg, Pennsylvania to become the Secretary and Treasurer of the Robinson Garage. This would be the local automobile dealership for cars and trucks for decades. He worked in the family business until 1952.

With the health of his father, James W. declining in 1937, Robinson's Garage, Incorporated (corporation) was legally dissolved and became a partnership and continued to do business at the same location and with the same owners about mid-year. This action would make it easier to transfer the business after the death of his father on February 22, 1938. Stewart would incorporate Robinson's Garage again on October 19, 1948.

In October 1953, Stewart applied for permission to operate a taxicab service in Saltsburg, Pennsylvania along with the Saltsburg Motor Company. This business venture did not pan out and terminated.

Stewart was highly active in the community. He was a member and had served as Treasurer of the Board of Trustees of the Saltsburg Presbyterian Church from 1942 to 1951. He served as the Treasurer of the Saltsburg Board of Trade and was a Director of the Saltsburg Area Development Corporation and a member of

Italian War Merit Cross

Above: Stewart and Eleanor in May 1982.

the Saltsburg Planning Corporation and a Director of the Saltsburg Area Recreation Association from 1958 to 1975. Also, he was a member of the Indiana Hospital, had been the First Vice President of the William Penn Council of the Boy Scouts of America from 1958 until 1966 and had served as the First Vice President and Chairperson of the Indiana County United Fund. He was selected as the Citizen of the Week in Pittsburgh, Pennsylvania in 1962.

He was a charter and life member (Fifty year member) of the Saltsburg Lions Club. He was honored in 1980 as the only active charter member of the Lions Club. Also, he was a charter and life member of the Veterans of Foreign Wars (VFW) Post 1989 of Indiana and was a member of the Saltsburg American Legion Post 57.

As a First Lieutenant with the U. S. Army during World War I, he received the Italian War Merit Cross Decoration (Croce of Merito di Guerra). (Note: This medal was instituted by King Victor Emanuel in 1918 and was awarded to members of the armed forces with a minimum of one year service who had been in contact with the enemy, or to those who, when mentioned for war merit, received a promotion. This medal is given to Italian military personnel only; however, the Italian government made an exception and awarded the medal to members of the Foggiani)

He would receive a veteran's compensation for twenty months at a rate of $10 per month starting in 1934.

He married his wife, Eleanor McClelland Robinson on July 6, 1948. Eleanor was born on January 1, 1908, and was a graduate of Indiana University of Pennsylvania and had taught school in Connellsville, Pennsylvania for nineteen years and then several years in the Saltsburg schools. She died at the age of eighty-four years on July 31, 1992.

Stewart died at the age of ninety-one years on Sunday, October 6, 1985.

Stewart was quite a guy – an intelligent, brave, adventurous man with a profound sense of humor. When you look back on his life, Stewart was on track for a career in the banking and finance world after graduating from Princeton and then the war took him in a different direction. During the war not only was Stewart to become a member of the famous "Foggiani" but he lived and played a significant part in the evolution of "machines." He was a trailblazer in two industries: airplanes and automobiles. He was among the first to participate in the military use of aviation and participated in the development of airplanes. He flew some of the original aircraft built after the Wright brothers demonstrated that man could fly. And then he was on the ground floor in the development of the automobile industry. He operated one of the first automobile dealerships in rural America and demonstrated new methods to advertise and sell automobiles. In today's terms, he was at the forefront of not one but two significant industries that we rely on heavily today!

Stewart was a favorite uncle with his nieces and nephews and at the family Christmas gatherings, he would always give them a little "pin money," as he called it, which was usually a five- or ten-dollar bill. Friends and family members would describe him as follows: "If you never met him, you could always pick out Stewart in a crowd of people because he was always looking dapper with a real twinkle in his eyes and a great sense of humor."

Above: An SVA 5 of 87a Squadriglia..

Above: Restored Ansaldo A.1 Balilla 16553.

Acknowledgements

First and foremost, I would like to thank Shannon Monich for presenting to me the journals of Samuel Stewart Robinson. These journals gave me the opportunity to share his experiences and exploits during World War One. Keep in mind that these journals are over one hundred years old and some of the ink has faded and the pages are worn, but the journals are in great condition otherwise. Stories about firsthand experiences during the war are very rare and provide such great insight into an aviator's life abroad that these veterans had to endure.

I would like to thank my niece Danielle Sagan and my partner, Diane Barr, for assisting me in transcribing the journals.

Through the numerous edits, my daughter Brianne Sagan and my partner, Diane Barr and my sister, Nancy Summers, gave me invaluable advice and edit suggestions to help tell Stewart's story.

Members of Over the Front, especially Michael O'Neal, Dr. James Streckfuss, and Charlie Walthall for their valuable input.

Finally, Diana Flinn, Rebecca Lydic, Christina Simpson (Lytle) for sharing some personal stories and anticdotes about Stewart.

Above: The ISVA was a floatplane fighter conversion of the speedy SVA 5. The floats had hydrofoils to assist take-off.

Glossary of Terms

American 2.M. – American Military Markets.

Boches – a German soldier; a disparaging and offensive term; a contemptuous term used to refer to a German, especially a German soldier in World War One.

Brevets – In the military, a brevet is a warrant that gives a commissioned officer a higher rank title as a reward, but which may not confer the authority and privileges of real rank. Originally a French Air Service term that indicates that a cadet had completed a prescribed course of flight instruction and was designated a military pilot. The Italian brevet is the hardest to get in the world. After getting the 1st brevet and the 2nd brevet, it then entitles the aviator to wear the golden Italian eagle.

BVD's – men's long one-piece long underwear; long undergarments for men; Bradley, Voorhees, and Day are the manufacturer.

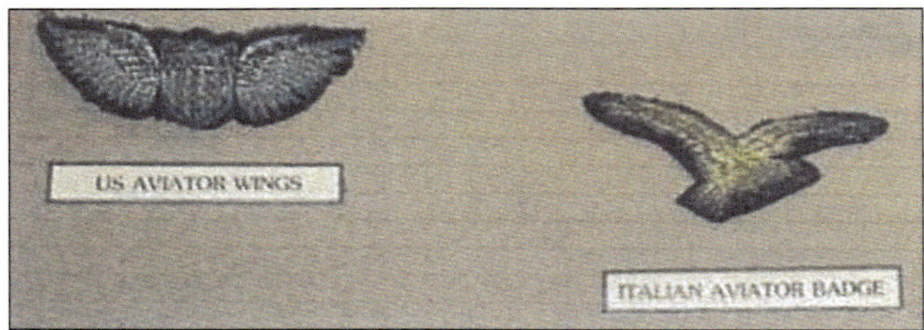

Caproni-3 - was the mainstay of the Italian bomber fleet. The crew of four were in an open central nacelle (not really a "cockpit", but simply a large open compartment. The forward machine gunner was at the very front of the ship. Behind him sat the two pilots. The tail gunner was at the back of the nacelle, mounted on a platform above the number three engine, which drove the pusher prop. The bomb load was suspended beneath the hull.

Caproni

Caudrons – was designed by René and Gaston Caudron as a development of their earlier Caudron G.2 for military use. It first flew in May 1914 at their Le Crotoy aerodrome. The aircraft had a short crew nacelle, with a single engine in the nose of the nacelle, and an open tail boom truss. It was of sesquiplane layout, and used wing warping for lateral control, although this was replaced by conventional ailerons fitted on the upper wing in late production aircraft. Usually, the G.3 was not armed, although sometimes light machine guns and small bombs were fitted.

It was ordered in massive quantities following the outbreak of the First World War with the Caudron factories building 1423 of the 2450 built in France and 233 were also built in England and 166 built in Italy along with several other countries. The Caudron brothers did not charge a licensing fee for the design, as an act of patriotism.

Caudron G.3

Farman – is a French aircraft developed before One by the Farman Aviation Works. It was used as a reconnaissance and light bomber during the early part of World War One, later being relegated to training duties. A pusher configuration unequal-span biplane like the earlier Farman MF.7, the MF.11 differed in lacking the forward-mounted elevator, the replacement of the biplane horizontal tail surfaces with a single surface with a pair of rudders mounted above it, and the mounting of the nacelle containing crew and engine in the gap between the two wings. The aircraft was also fitted with a machine gun for the observer, whose position was changed from the rear seat to the front to give a clear field of fire.

Foggia, Italy is a province in the Apulia region of Italy. This province is also known as **Daunia**, after the Daunians, an Iapygian pre-Roman tribe living in Tavoliere plain, and as **Capitanata**, derived from *Catapanata*, since the area was governed by a catepan as part of the Catepanate of Italy during the High Middle Ages. Its capital is the city of Foggia.

Foggiani – term used to refer to American military aviators who were trained in Foggia, Italy during World War One at the Eight Aviation Instruction Center.

Huns - was a derogatory term used by the British and Americans to describe German soldiers during the First World War.

Pomlio – the Italians called this machine "casa di morta" or house of death.
Reuilly, France – is a commune in the Indre department in central France. It is about fifteen km south of Vierzon, and thirty km west of Bourges. The area around Reuilly is noted for its wine; there is a designated Reuilly AOC.

Pomilio PD

S.A.I. 7B – a bi-plane ordered from the Societa Italiana Aviazone, an affiliate of the Fiat motor car company. It was one of several machines used for training at Foggia.

Sam Brown Belts – is a wide leather belt with a narrow supporting strap that passes over the right shoulder, worn by military and police officers. Worn by most officers overseas during World War One. It is named after Sir Samuel J. Browne (1824–1901), the British Indian Army general who invented it.

SIA 7B2

Tommies – known as a slang term for British soldiers of the First World War. During the war, French and German troops would all refer to British soldiers as "Tommies" and phrases like "For you Tommy the war is over" had become synonymous with British Forces.

Sam Brown Belt

WOP - is a pejorative slur for Italians.

References

- "Dear Bert," An American Pilot flying in World War I Italy, by Edward Davis Lewis, February 2002.
- "A Brief History of the United States School of Military Aeronautics at Princeton University," by Michael O'Neal.
- "Letters from a World War I Aviator," by Josiah P. Rowe, Jr. September 1986.
- "Journal of S. Stewart Robinson from October 13, 1917, to June 3, 1918", written Samuel Stewart Robinson.
- "Journal of S. Stewart Robinson from June 4, 1918, to October 2, 1918", written Samuel Stewart Robinson
- "Journal of S. Stewart Robinson from October 3, 1918, to February 5, 1919", written Samuel Stewart Robinson.
- The aviation museum in Stavanger is restoring a Caproni Ca.310. The picture is the reconstruction of the Caproni cockpit. Photo credit: Kjetil Dahle.
- Google Maps, 2018, Inst. Geogr. Nacional.
- Various pictures, documents, maps, etc. from Michael O'Neal.

Above: SIA 9B 10796. Larger than its sibling SIA 7B reconniassance plane, the 9B was a bomber with a 700 hp FIAT A.14 engine, the most powerful aero engine to see service in WWI. After it dropped its bombs it could out pace any enemy fighter. Unfortunately, it inherited the same weak wings as the 7B and only a few saw service.

Above: Pomilio PE was a development of the PD with nose radiator.

Made in the USA
Middletown, DE
27 March 2025

73127879R00071